customizing
clothes

from dull to divine in 30 projects

Kate Haxell

INTERWEAVE PRESS
www.interweave.com

First edition published in the United States by

Interweave Press LLC
201 East Fourth Street
Loveland, CO 80537-5655 USA
www.interweave.com

Printed and bound in China

Library of Congress Cataloging-in-Publication Data

Haxell, Kate.
    Customizing cool clothes : from dull to divine
in 30 projects / Kate Haxell.
        p. cm.
    Includes index.
    ISBN 10: 1-59668-015-6 (pbk.)
    ISBN 13: 978-1-59668-015-9 (pbk.)
    1. Fancy work. 2. Clothing and dress. I. Title.
TT750.H39 2006
746—dc22

                            2006012373

    10 9 8 7 6 5 4 3 2 1

Dedication
For Jackie, who taught me to sew.

contents

Introduction

Do you open your closet door every day and feel your heart sink? Do you stare wistfully into the windows of high-end boutiques and just know that you would look fabulous in that silver beaded miniskirt, the one you can't afford? Do you wish desperately for something sparkling and sequined to liven up your party outfit? Here in your hands is the answer to your wishes.

Customizing Cool Clothes shows you, step by simple step, how to turn inexpensive, mass-produced garments into one-off designer originals that let you dress to impress. The book starts with some basic techniques, so if you're a needlework novice, there's no need to worry. The equipment needed is basic and the techniques easy to learn. Sections on sourcing embellishments and choosing the right ones for your garments will help you make brilliant creative choices, and then it's on to the projects!

Whether your style is Bohemian, classic, retro, or edgy, there are projects in this book to suit you. Even if you're a beginner to sewing, you can work some magic on a plain T-shirt (see Cute Puppy T-shirt, page 36), or add style to dull denim jeans (see Rickrack Jeans, page 28). There are also lots of ideas for keen stitchers and beaders, from glittering beaded embroidery (see Beaded Flower Blouse, page 54) to a tulle and ribbon overskirt that will completely transform a plain skirt (see Glamorous Party Skirt, page 81).

Each project starts with an easy-to-find chain-store garment—denim jeans, a velvet jacket, or a flared skirt—so it's simple for you to adapt the ideas to fit your own clothes, and there's plenty of advice on doing so. The trimmings and embellishments used are also widely available— some frayed silk, a few sequins, vintage buttons, bits of fabric, and lengths of ribbon. Detailed materials lists, with tips on measuring your garment, mean that you can buy just what you need to complete a project, and clear step-by-step photographs and instructions guide you through every stage of the transformation.

Customizing your clothes is not just cool, it's also creative, fun, and inspiring. I'm sure you'll love doing it as much as I do.

Kate Haxell

Equipment

Very little equipment is needed to do any of the projects in this book, and it is likely that you will already have most of what you do need. On these pages are the basic items you will need with some notes and tips you will find useful.

NEEDLES

Hand sewing needles come in a wide variety of shapes and sizes, but many are designed for special tasks, and you can safely ignore them. It is difficult to give needle sizes for the projects in this book, as the garments you may be working on may well be made from a different fabric or of a different weight to those used here. However, good general advice is to choose a needle that slips easily through the fabric you are sewing, without leaving a hole, and the eye must be large enough to take the thread you are using. You can buy needle threaders that will help with this latter task. When embroidering jersey fabric (for example, Flower Tank, page 32), choose the finest embroidery needle you have. Whatever the type of needle, the higher the size number, the shorter and thinner the needle is with a few exceptions.

An old needle is probably a blunt needle, so don't keep using the one that has been sitting in your needle cushion for years. If it snags on the fabric, throw it away and use a new one.

Sewing machine needles also come in different types and sizes, but you just need a general-purpose one for these projects. Again, change them as soon as they start to snag or become blunt.

PINS

I like to use long pins with glass heads so that I can see them easily. If you are sewing very fine fabrics, then silk pins—which are thinner—will help you avoid marking the fabric.

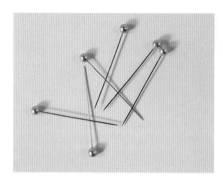

Long glass-headed pins.

SEWING MACHINE

If you don't have a machine, see if you can borrow one—you won't need it for long as none of the projects in this book are time-consuming. If you are going to buy your own machine, there's no need to spend a lot of money. I use a basic machine, as the only stitches I need are straight stitch and zigzag stitch. A one-stop buttonhole maker is worth having, if you are going to do a lot of sewing—it does make life (or at least, buttonholes) easier.

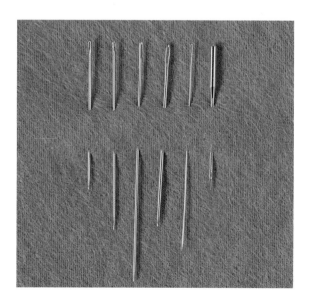

Left to right: Sharps sewing needle, size 5; these needles come in sizes 1–12, with 1 being the longest and thickest. Milliners needle; these are very long slim needles and are my personal favorites for nearly all kinds of hand sewing. They slip easily through fabric and their length makes them easy to handle. Long darner; these very long needles are thicker than milliners needles, but are useful for basting as you can stitch quickly along. Embroidery needle, size 1; this larger size of embroidery needle is easy to thread but may be too thick for lightweight fabrics. Beading needle, size 13; this is the largest of the commonly available beading needles, and the one I use most of the time. Sewing machine needle, 12/80; this is a general-purpose sized needle that you can use for all the projects in this book.

FABRIC MARKERS

There are different types of these available, but I generally use either a vanishing marker or a chalk pencil. It depends how strong the mark needs to be and what the fabric is. Whichever marker you use, always check on a discreet corner of the fabric that the mark will disappear without trace.

Top: Vanishing marker; the marks made with this fade away after a short time.
Above: Chalk pencils; the marks from these are brushed off once the sewing is complete. Different colors are useful for marking different-colored fabrics.

RULERS AND TAPE MEASURE

Rulers are useful for measuring small areas of flat fabric and for turning up hems. My absolute favorite is a small 6-inch (15-cm) ruler. It lives in my sewing box and gets used all the time. However, a conventional 12-inch (30-cm) ruler, just like the ones you had at school, will do just as well.

Use a cloth tape measure for measuring around areas (such as the bottom of a skirt) and for long lengths. When choosing a tape measure, buy one that has the measurements starting right at the end. I once had one that started a short distance from the end and I was forever forgetting and cutting things to the wrong length—very annoying.

Top: Short 6-inch (15-cm) metal ruler.
Center above: Long 12-inch (30-cm) ruler.
Below: Cloth tape measure.

Above: Dressmaker's scissors.
Right: Embroidery scissors.

SCISSORS

These are the only pieces of equipment that are worth spending some money on. Buy the best you can afford and never ever use them for cutting anything other than fabric or thread; even thin paper will blunt them quickly. Buy a large pair of dressmaker's scissors for cutting fabric and a small pair of embroidery scissors for snipping threads and cutting small details.

Techniques

You don't have to be a skilled sewer to attempt any of the projects in this book, and many of the projects are very forgiving of complete beginners. If you are unsure of a particular technique, practice first on a scrap of fabric (ideally of a similar weight to your project), before you start.

MATCHING THREADS TO FABRICS

Commercially made garments are sewn with threads that are dyed to match the fabric exactly. This option isn't available to home sewers, but there is a vast range of thread colors available, and it is nearly always possible to find a good match. If you can't find a perfect match, then choose a thread that is a shade darker than the fabric, rather than one that is lighter, because a darker thread will show less.

The same rule applies when choosing a thread for a patterned fabric— choose one that matches the darkest color in the pattern.

Far left: This is a good thread to fabric match.
Center: This thread matches the darkest color in the patterned fabric.
Below: When choosing thread to sew on ribbon (see Attaching Ribbon, page 12), you need to match the thread color to the ribbon color. This ribbon is striped, so two threads (one for each side) are needed.

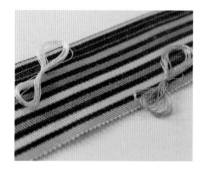

USING A SEWING MACHINE

If you are unfamiliar with the sewing machine you are using, read the instruction book first, then practice on different scraps of fabric before sewing a project. If the stitches are loose, adjust the thread tension until the stitches are flat and even. If the machine is missing stitches, change the needle. When sewing, place your hands flat on the machine bed either side of the needle, and as close to it as feels comfortable. Do be careful not to sew your fingers, it hurts!

Don't just press the pedal and let the fabric run through the machine, use your hands to guide it. This does take a bit of practice, but it will make your sewing look much better.

Remove pins as you reach them when sewing; don't try to sew over them or you can break the machine needle or pin and bunch up or damage your fabric.

The plate of the machine (the metal piece under the needle) has measurements on it, marking off the distance from the needle when it is in the central position. Keeping the edge of the fabric running against the appropriate measurement will give you an even seam.

The edge of the fabric is against a measurement on the plate.

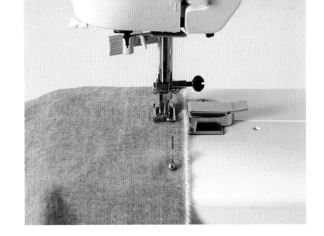

However, if you find it hard to keep the seam even, invest in a magnetic seam guide. (Note that this is not advised for digital sewing machines.) This is a handy little magnet with a straight edge that sits on the metal plate wherever you put it. Place it on the measurement you want to follow and let the edge of the fabric run along the guide. It is much easier to see and to control the seam width.

The edge of the fabric is against the edge of the magnetic seam guide.

SECURING THREADS

I was taught never to knot threads at the end of a line of stitching, as a knot can come undone eventually. I still follow this good advice and pass it on to you. Instead, start and finish a line of machine stitching by reversing a few stitches. Most machines have a lever or button that allows you to do this. Trim the ends of the threads short when the sewing is complete.

If you are hand stitching, then you can start stitching with a knot tied at the end of the thread. Make the knot big enough not to pull through the fabric. The best way to secure the ends of threads is with a few tiny backstitches in a discreet place. Either make the stitches within the seam allowance or under an embellishment on the front of the fabric where they won't show.

Similarly, when you need a line of machine stitching to end very neatly (for example, if you are topstitching and the line of stitches will show on the front of the fabric), secure the threads by hand. Pull the thread on the front through to the back, thread a needle with both ends (or one at a time, if this is easier) and then make the tiny backstitches. Go back to the start of the line of stitching and secure the threads in the same way.

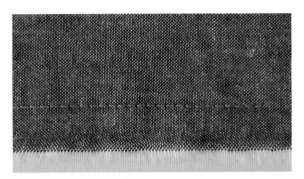

This line of stitching is finished with a few reverse stitches. It is secure and almost invisible.

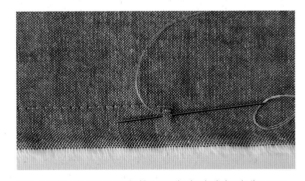

Here, the threads are secured with some tiny backstitches in the seam allowance.

ATTACHING TRIMMINGS TO A HEMMED EDGE

When sewing a trimming with a selvedge to the back of a garment, it is important that the stitches do not show on the front, or the work will look untidy. If the edge of the garment has no hem, then this cannot be done and it is better to use an alternative trim. However, if it has a hem, then follow these instructions. The technique may seem complicated, but it is very easy to do once you get into the rhythm—try it and see for yourself.

1 Thread a sewing needle with sewing thread that matches the garment fabric and knot one end. To stitch the top edge of a selvedge, make a tiny straight stitch through the back of the hem where you want to start attaching the trimming. Slip the needle through a few strands on the front of the selvedge at the start of the trimming. Make another tiny stitch through the back of the hem, just next to the first stitch, and pull gently on the thread to bring the hem and trimming together. *Slip the needle through the hem, making sure it doesn't appear on the front of the garment, to emerge about ¼ inch (5 mm) farther along. Make a stitch through the front of the selvedge ¼ inch (5 mm) from the first stitch and pull the thread taut. Do not pull so tightly that you pucker the fabric. Repeat from * to attach the rest of the trimming.

2 If the selvedge is wide, stitch the lower edge in place as well, to avoid it rolling up and showing over the hem. The principle is the same, but you catch a thread in the bottom edge of the selvedge with the needle, rather than threads in the front.

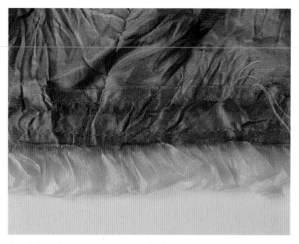

Attaching trimmings to a hemmed edge If you stitch on the trimming neatly, no stitches should show on the front of the garment.

Attaching trimmings to knitted fabric When worked through a seam stitch, the sewing that holds the trimming in place is invisible.

Attaching flat trimmings Attach flat trimmings with tiny stitches.

ATTACHING TRIMMINGS TO KNITTED FABRIC

One thing to bear in mind when trimming knitwear is that the stitching and the trimming itself will reduce the elasticity of the fabric. The best rule to follow is not to trim an edge that must be stretched in order to get into the garment.

If the knitted fabric has a hem, then you can sew the trimming's selvedge to it in the same way as for a hemmed fabric (see opposite page). If the selvedge is narrow, then follow the technique below.

1 Thread a sewing needle with sewing thread that matches the knitted fabric and knot one end. Make a tiny stitch over the seam stitch of the knitted fabric to anchor the thread. From the front, make a stitch through the bottom edge of the selvedge. *From below, take the needle through the seam stitch of the fabric, as shown, 1/4 inch (5 mm) farther along. From the front, take the needle through the bottom edge of the selvedge 1/4 inch (5 mm) from the first stitch and pull the thread taut. Do not pull so tightly that you pucker the fabric. Repeat from * to attach the rest of the trimming.

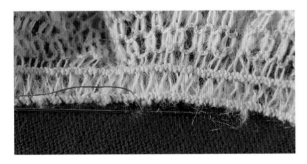

2 If you are sewing the trimming to a section of knitted fabric that doesn't have a seam stitch, or if the seam stitch is too close to the edge, the stitches will show as a series of tiny depressions on the front of the garment. However, this is usually tidy enough and is quite acceptable. Use the same technique, but carefully take the needle through the backs of two or three knitted stitches, rather than through the seam stitch.

ATTACHING FLAT TRIMMINGS

A decorative trimming is best attached to the front of a garment by hand. You can machine stitch it in place, but the stitching will show and can spoil the look of the garment. The precise way in which a trimming is sewn on will vary depending on the style of the trimming itself, but the principle is the same.

1 Lay the trimming in position on the garment. If you find it easier, you can pin or baste it in place. Thread a sewing needle with sewing thread that matches the trimming and knot one end. From the back, bring the needle through the fabric to where you want to start attaching the trimming. *Make a tiny stitch through the trimming or, as here, over a section of it, depending on its style. Return the needle through the fabric and bring it back out 1/4 inch (5 mm) past the first stitch or at the next appropriate point on the trimming. If you are sewing trimming on top of a hem, slip the needle through the hem for neatness. Repeat from * to attach the rest of the trimming.

ATTACHING RIBBON

To do this really well you need to master using the sewing machine (see page 8), as the more accurate your machine stitching is, the better the finished result will look. I always baste ribbon in place before machine stitching it, as I find that pins do not hold it accurately or flat enough.

1 Pin and then baste the ribbon to the garment. To baste, thread a sewing needle with a sewing thread that is a very different color to the ribbon so that you can see the stitches easily to remove them afterwards. Make running stitches ¼ inch (5 mm) in from the edges of the ribbon so that they don't get caught up in the machine stitching. Don't worry about making the stitches even, they are just there to hold the ribbon temporarily in place.

2 Thread the sewing machine with a thread that matches the ribbon and set it to a medium-length straight stitch. Starting at one end, machine stitch one side of the ribbon to the garment, making the line of stitching as close as possible to the edge of the ribbon, but without going over the edge onto the garment fabric. Stitch slowly, keeping an even pressure on the machine pedal, and keeping your eyes on the ribbon. If you need to stop stitching, do so with the needle down into the fabric to prevent it moving. When you reach the end of the ribbon, secure the threads (see page 9).

3 Return to the starting point and machine stitch the other side of the ribbon, stitching in the same direction as for the first edge. This is important as it helps to prevent the ribbon puckering. If you need to stitch across the short ends, do this after you have stitched the long edges. Once all the machine stitching is complete, remove the basting threads.

CHAIN STITCH

This simple embroidery stitch can be very useful in spicing up a utilitarian garment. Choose an embroidery needle that slips easily through your fabric (see Needles, page 6). Cut a length of six-strand embroidery floss, split it into two three-strand lengths, and work with one of them.

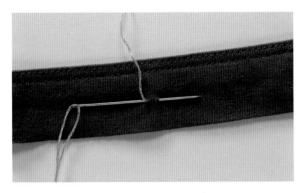

1 Thread the needle with a three-strand length of floss and knot one end. From the back, bring the needle through the fabric at the starting point. Return it through the fabric close to where it came out and make a short straight stitch; do not pull the needle through.

3 Pull the needle through the fabric and gently pull the floss taut.

2 Loop the floss under the point of the needle.

4 Take the needle back down where it came out at the top of the loop and make a short straight stitch. Repeat Steps 1–4 to work chain stitch. Change the angle of the straight stitches to change direction and vary the length to make short or long chain stitches.

Chain stitch is both quick and easy to work, and it looks great, too.

BEADED BLANKET STITCH

This is a lovely way of adding sparkle to the edge of a garment or ribbon.
It may seem tedious, but it does proceed surprisingly quickly once you get
into the rhythm. To work plain blanket stitch, just omit the beads.

1 Thread the beading needle with a long length of thread and knot one end. From the back, take the needle through the fabric, very close to the edge. Take it through again in the same direction and same place to make a tiny straight stitch over the edge of the fabric. Slip the needle under the top edge of this stitch and pull the thread through to start the blanket stitch.

3 Wrap the thread under the point of the needle, making sure the bead doesn't slip down the thread.

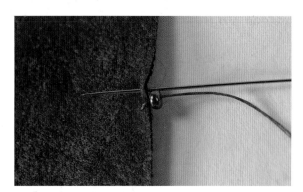

2 Pick up a bead and slide it down the thread to sit next to the fabric edge. Take the needle through the fabric, very close to the edge and a bead's width from the previous stitch.

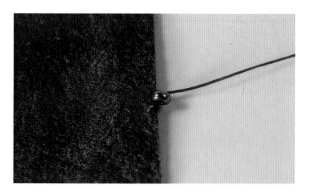

4 Pull the needle through and pull the thread taut so that the bead sits on the edge of the fabric. Repeat Steps 2–4 to work beaded blanket stitch.

With just a little practice, it is easy to work
beautifully neat, beaded blanket stitch.

LAUNDERING

You will find that most store-bought embellished garments specify hand-washing or dry-cleaning only, and the same will apply to most garments you embellish yourself. When choosing embellishments, check to see if they have any laundering instructions (though annoyingly most don't). Careful hand-washing will overcome most problems, but if you are concerned, sew a scrap of the embellishment onto a discrete corner of the garment and wash it to check the results.

When ironing embellished garments, proceed carefully. Never iron sequins because they will curl up and shrivel. If you have scraps of the fabrics left over from a project, test the iron temperature on them first.

Your version of Pretty Patched Trousers (see page 104) is a garment that will almost definitely need to be hand-washed or dry-cleaned, as it will combine a mixture of different fabrics and motifs.

Sourcing embellishments

Finding the trimmings, beads, ribbons, and sequins needed to transform dull garments into wonderful, original pieces that you'll wear with pride is the first step in your customizing adventure.

There are many sources for these desirable items and two ways to acquire them. The first way is, some might say, the sensible way. Pick the item you want to work on and take it to the shops with you to choose the perfect decoration.

The second method is more random, takes up more space, and is more expensive, but it is so very appealing. Every time you see something you like, buy it. You will quickly assemble a collection of gorgeous items in your favorite colors and styles—a collection you can raid whenever the urge to customize hits you. I favor this method and have cupboards and drawers full of lovely things to prove it. However, sometimes you just won't have the perfect embellishment, so then it's certainly time to be sensible and take your garment shopping.

If you are buying things as you see them, try to buy sensible, useable amounts. I always pick bags of about 500 beads or 100 sequins, choose at least ten buttons of a type, and buy a minimum of 2 yards (2 m) of a trimming or ribbon. There is always the danger that you might not have enough for a certain project, but it's bound to be enough for something else, and there's nothing more frustrating than remembering something you once saw and would now like, only to find that you can no longer get it.

Having said this, you do need to exercise a certain amount of discipline, otherwise you can easily end up with an extensive and expensive horde of treasures that you never use. Most of us have favorite colors and preferred styles of clothing. We know what suits us and what doesn't. Keep your colors and styles in your mind when shopping. There's no point in buying the most fabulous mauve marabou feathers if the color makes you look sallow and you don't ever wear girly things.

Start your collecting by casting a wide net. Visit local notions, bead, and craft stores, rummage through thrift shops, go to craft and sewing fairs, wander around flea markets, and browse that marvelous tool, the Internet. Keep your eyes open for bargains and for the unexpected.

Look at vintage garments in terms of the elements they offer, rather than the whole thing. A secondhand evening dress in an ugly fabric may have beautiful beads that can be cut off. Clothes such as shirts and full skirts often have areas of fabric without seams that are large enough to make patches or trim cuffs. You can find bags of old buttons containing a few treasures that make it worth buying the bag and passing on what you don't want to a friend who can pick his or her favorites and pass it on in turn. Trimmings can be removed, handwashed, and ironed—ready to be used again. The more items you look at, the better your eyes will get at spotting the flowers among the weeds.

Do look at trimmings in furnishing shops, too. Trimmings are usually too heavy for thin fabrics (see Choosing Embellishments, page 18), but you can sometimes get really unusual, exciting pieces that are great for winter or outdoor garments.

Craft and sewing fairs are excellent places for some serious shopping. There will usually be a wide variety of items to choose from, and you may get some bargains from retailers offering special show discounts, particularly if you go on the last day. The only drawback to big fairs can be the vast number of other people also shopping.

The Internet can be a great resource, particularly if you don't have good local notions, bead, and craft shops. However, I find it difficult to judge color and quality of items from the often tiny pictures on the websites. There's nothing quite like being able to feel something before you buy. Therefore, I find that I tend to use the Internet to buy things I've seen elsewhere, but which are being offered online at a lower price.

Whichever shopping method and venues you use, have fun buying your embellishments—it shouldn't ever be a chore.

1. My trimmings box includes pieces salvaged from old clothes, "must-haves" bought in stores and at fairs, and some pieces people have given me as they've learned of my ever-growing collection.

2. I love the color lilac and so over time I've assembled a large collection of beads and sequins that are either that color or coordinate beautifully with it.

3. Ribbons are a versatile embellishment, and they are usually inexpensive. My stash includes lovely pieces of ribbon that I've saved from gifts—those given to me and to other people!

4. Customizing doesn't often require large lengths of fabric, so a collection of small pieces is a useful resource. This stack has pieces cut from shirt backs, remnants bought from stores, and pieces left over from dressmaking projects.

5. I adore vintage buttons and have a large collection of them. Check garments in flea markets for interesting finds, though you may end up throwing the garment itself away and just keeping the buttons!

6. Become a saver of bits and pieces of all sorts—you never know when they'll be just what you're seeking. Sew-on patches from old clothes, shisha mirrors, pom-poms cut off a furnishing trim, and sparkling plastic "gems" are just some of my treasures.

7. Faux flowers and leaves, and feathers of all sorts are versatile decorations that will find a home in lots of different customizing projects.

Choosing embellishments

The projects in this book have details of the plain garments and the embellishments used, as well as illustrated step-by-step instructions. However, it is likely that your garments will vary from the ones shown, and you may want to use different trimmings. This is fine, as the projects offer advice on adapting them. However, there is general advice on choosing embellishments that will help you achieve a more professional-looking result, so read these pages before you start customizing.

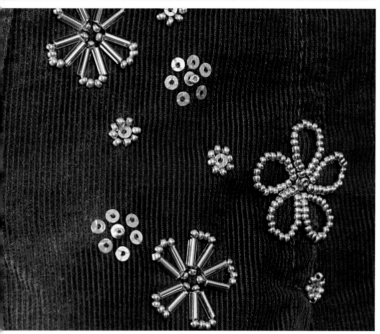

Above: Sequins offer a fabulous way of adding glamour to a garment and will turn a plain top into a party piece. These large cup sequins are particularly effective, as they reflect lots of light and so produce lots of sparkle. However, each one has to be sewn on individually by hand, so I recommend avoiding tiny sequins, unless you are going to use them very sparingly or are very patient. Large sequins will cover fabric surprisingly quickly, so it really doesn't take long to decorate a collar (see Sparkle Sequin Bolero Jacket, page 59). Sequins are lightweight, so they can be stitched onto fine fabrics without pulling the garment out of shape.

Left: Beading is a hugely popular craft, and many of its followers find it completely addictive. However, nonbeaders can be dismayed by how tiny the beads are and think that any project will take hours to complete. Don't worry, the bead projects in this book are designed with novices in mind, as well as bead addicts (see Beaded Miniskirt, page 62, and Beaded Flower Blouse, page 54). When considering beading a garment, remember beads in large quantities can be quite heavy and pull fine fabrics out of shape. It is also more difficult to bead lightweight fabrics without puckering occurring, so if you are beading for the first time, work on a medium-weight fabric such as corduroy or thick cotton.

Right: Buttons can make or break any garment. The most beautiful garment can be let down by cheap plastic buttons. One of the quickest and easiest ways to spice up a garment is to change the original buttons for carefully chosen alternatives (see Toggled Cargo Shorts, page 51).

However, buttons are also decorative in their own right and can be used to add gorgeous detail to a plain garment. They don't have to all match, indeed they often work better if they don't. Sticking to a simple color palette is a good idea, or your finished garment can look a little too crazy (see Silky Pashmina, page 119, and Vintage Button Trousers, page 49). Buttons will add weight, so don't sew a lot of them onto a fine fabric or you can distort the lines of the garment.

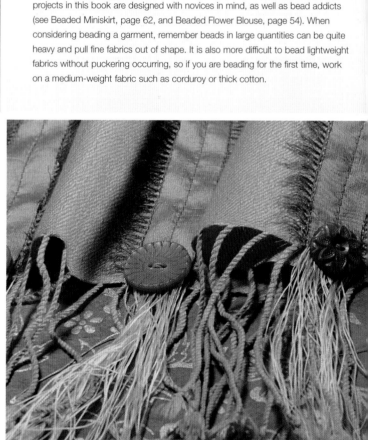

Right: There is a vast range of commercially available trimmings from which to choose, and some are horribly expensive. When picking a trimming, consider the humbler, inexpensive varieties, too. For example, simple rickrack comes in lots of colors, is widely available, and doesn't cost very much at all (see Rickrack Jeans, page 28). Remember that once a store has cut a length of trimming they won't refund your money, if you change your mind. So think carefully before buying something costly. However, sometimes the expensive trimming is the perfect one, so you just have to bite the bullet and buy it. If the trimming turns out to be more costly than the chain-store garment you are sewing it to, you can console yourself with the knowledge that the finished result will look fabulous and no one will ever guess its lowly origins.

When choosing a trimming for a garment, bear a couple of things in mind. First, are you able to sew it on successfully? Is the trimming of a suitable weight for the garment fabric, both practically and aesthetically? A heavy braid on the cuffs of a thin cotton shirt will drag the sleeves down and spoil the shape, while a light ruffled organza trimming on a thick velvet jacket can just look ridiculous.

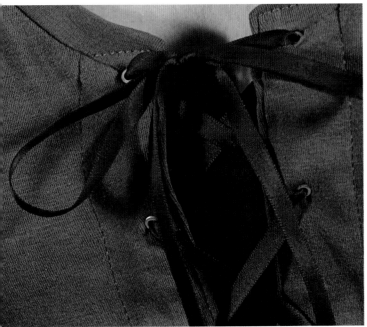

Below: We usually think of ribbon as a flat thing, but it can be shaped to add three-dimensional relief and texture to a project (see Velvet Jacket, page 84, and Sparkle Sequin Bolero Jacket, page 59). However, these ideas are best worked with wider, stiffer types of ribbon, both from a practical and aesthetic point of view. Fine, narrow ribbon is quite difficult to form and stitch neatly without damaging or puckering it. It is also floppy and won't hold a shape well, tending to give the finished garment an untidy, rather forlorn look.

Above: Ribbons, like trimmings, are available in a multitude of colors, fabrics, patterns, and widths, though they are generally less expensive, so you don't have to worry so much about making a mistake. They are one of the most versatile of embellishments. Use them to fasten a garment (see Ribbon-laced T-shirt, page 94); to add color and detail (see Silky Ribbon Shirt, page 72); or to decorate plain fabric (see Glamorous Party Skirt, page 81).

Sewing ribbon perfectly flat onto fabric is maybe the trickiest technique to master (see Attaching Ribbon, page 12), so do practice this before you start one of the projects that requires it. The vast majority of ribbons are lightweight, so they can be stitched to fine fabric without fear.

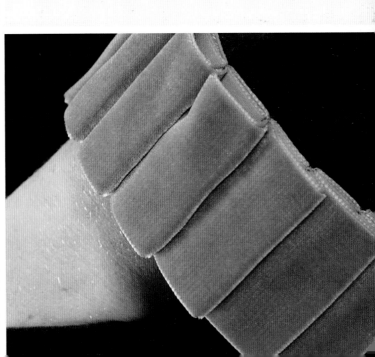

Right: Sew-on fabric motifs are a boon to the enthusiastic customizer. There is a reasonably wide range available and they are very quick and easy to use. Some are quite extravagant and include beading and embroidery, while other plainer types can easily be made more decorative, if need be, with some simple stitching (see Flower Camisole, page 35). Most are lightweight and so can be stitched onto any garment. There are iron-on types available, but I'm never confident of their ability to withstand laundering, so I always add a few stitches as well as ironing them, just to be sure.

Left: Sew-ons are also available in materials other than fabric, such as plastic, metal, and mirror. These are brilliant for adding sparkle to a garment, but be aware of their weight and the fabric you want to sew them to. Lightweight plastic "gems" work well even on quite fine fabrics (see Pink Jewel Sweater, page 41), as do shisha mirrors, but some of the metal and rhinestone motifs are better confined to heavier weight fabrics, such as denim.

Right: Using fabrics to customize clothes is usually cost-effective, as most projects don't require much yardage. As with trimmings, stores won't refund money on a cut length unless it has a fault in it, so before you buy, work out how much you need. If you find this complicated, cut the pieces you need out of newspaper and lay them out on the floor to assess the minimum amount of fabric needed. If you are going to hunt for a remnant to use in a project, take your newspaper shapes with you and lay them on the fabric to check that the piece is large enough. When buying a patterned fabric, think about how you want to position the design motifs, as this may affect how much you need to buy.

The weight and texture of the fabric needs to be considered, too. If the garment is lightweight, avoid sewing heavy fabrics to it as they may spoil the shape. Textured fabrics, such as velvet and fur, can add tactile glamour to plain garments (see Leopard Jeans, page 120, and Retro Furry Cardigan, page 108).

Storing embellishments

Having assembled your collection of irresistible trimmings, ribbons, and beads, you do need to store them in a practical way. If you just throw them in a cupboard or drawer, they will become horribly tangled and possibly lost. It'll be impossible to find anything, and items will be irretrievably damaged. There are lots of craft storage items on the market, but they are often expensive. A little ingenuity will produce equally practical and much cheaper storage solutions.

RIBBONS

These are serious offenders when it comes to tangling. Pinning them will work, but the pins can leave holes, and it is easy to stab yourself on them when hunting through the stash. I find the best solution is to use a pack of mini plastic clothespins (sold as a fun way to clip paperwork together) and a large box. I coil each length of ribbon and clip it together with a clothespins, and then store them in rows by color with each pin vertically upright in the box. They sit neatly and it's easy to find just the ribbon you need.

BEADS

These clever stackers (left) are the only specialist craft storage system I buy. They come in different sizes, and you can stack as many pots together as necessary. I keep my beads in stacks by color (other than the pearls, which all live together). When I'm working on a project, I make a special stack of the relevant beads so that I can find them all easily. These stackers are made by different manufacturers, so always make sure you buy the same brand, as not all the brands will fit together.

BUTTONS

I store my buttons by color in a collection of old jam jars. If you, want you can design labels for your jars, though I find it better to keep the jars blank so that I can see the contents easily.

TIED BUTTONS

The best way to keep sets of buttons together is to tie them with strong cotton thread or thin string. Be very good about always doing this, even if there are only two buttons the same, and you will always know exactly what you've got.

FABRICS

I find that the best way to store fabrics is in small, folded stacks, by color, on shelves. It's easy to see what you want and to lift the stack out to get the piece without pulling out other pieces. If you don't have this option, then a series of small, clear plastic, stacking crates is a good solution.

TRIMMINGS

As trimmings are bulky, they don't work so well with the clothespins I use for ribbons. However, trimmings tend to be less inclined to tie themselves in knots, so I keep mine coiled up and stored in old shoe boxes. You can arrange them by color or type, or any other system that works for you. Some trimmings can be quite delicate, so don't bundle them too tightly or put pins in them.

projects

trimmings

buttons and beads

ribbons

sewing

trimmings

ruffled vintage camisole

Pale brown camisole top with frayed edges and drawstring neckline.

With its crumpled finish and deliberately frayed edges, the silky fabric of this pretty, vintage-style camisole is perfectly complemented by the soft, looped ruffle of the organza trimming and sheen of the pearl beads. Confining the embellishment to the neckline keeps the look stylish, uncluttered, and very appealing.

you will need

- Sewing needle (see Needles, page 6)
- Sewing threads, pale brown and pale pink
- Organza ruffled trimming with selvedge, pale pink (see How Much?, below)
- Scissors, dressmaker's and embroidery
- Beading needle, size 13
- Beading thread, size D, pale brown
- Pearl disk beads, ¼-inch (5-mm) diameter, about 25
- Seed beads, size 10 or 11, pale pink
- Scrap of card stock (see Style Solutions, page 27)
- Pins

HOW MUCH?

You will need enough trimming to go around the camisole neckline, plus ¾ inch (2 cm) for the hems.

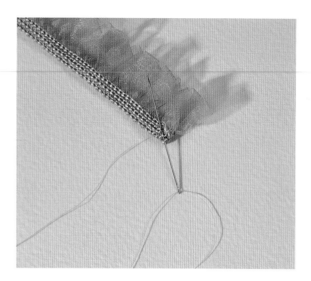

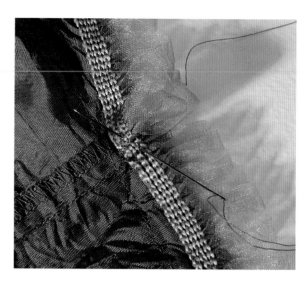

1 Turn under and stitch one short end of the trimming, using pale pink thread. Make the hem as small as possible to avoid bulkiness.

3 When the trimming is sewn in place, cut off most of the excess, leaving enough to turn under the remaining end, as in Step 1. The two short ends should butt closely together; stitch in place.

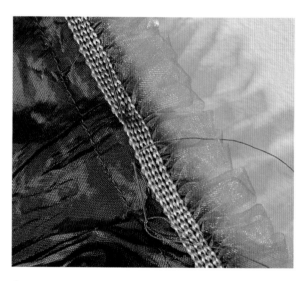

2 Starting with the hemmed end of the trimming at the center back of the camisole neckline and with the organza ruffles standing upright, pin the selvedge edge inside the camisole neckline. Using pale brown thread, slip stitch the top edge of the selvedge around the neckline. Slip the needle through the hem—or in this case, the drawstring channel—to avoid any stitches showing on the front of the camisole (see Attaching Trimmings to a Hemmed Edge, page 10). Remove pins.

4 Slip stitch the lower edge of the trimming in place to prevent it rolling forward.

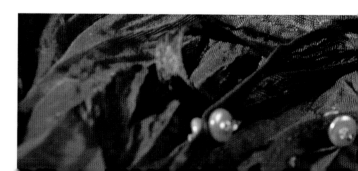

STYLE SOLUTIONS

The spacing of the pearl disks will depend on design elements of your chosen top. Here, the gap between the edges of the drawstring channel at the front of the camisole decided the spaces between the disks. Spend some time trying different spacings and check that the spaces will work out evenly right around the neckline. If necessary, measure and mark the positions of the disks with pins before you start sewing them on.

5 Thread the beading needle with a long length of beading thread and knot one end. Decide on the spacing of pearl disks and cut the card stock to a rectangle that is the length of the space between disks (see Style Solutions, above). Bring the needle from the back of the camisole fabric near the edge of the trimming to the position of the first disk and pick up one pearl disk and one seed bead. Return the needle back down through the disk and fabric at the same place it came out. Pull the thread tight to hold the disk and bead close to the fabric and make a tiny securing stitch on the back of the trimming.

6 Slip one end of the card stock under the edge of the first disk so that it sits against the thread. Take the needle through the drawstring channel and bring it up at the other end of the rectangle, ready to attach the next disk and bead. Continue in this manner until you have beaded around the neckline. Secure the thread (see Securing Threads, page 9).

7 Stitch one disk and bead to one of the drawstrings, positioning them 8 inches (20 cm) above the end. Bring the needle through to the opposite side of the drawstring, pick up another disk and bead, then take the needle back down through the disk and the drawstring. Secure the thread by knotting it around the base of the first disk and trim the end. Repeat for the other drawstring.

rickrack jeans

Denim jeans with flat fell outside leg seams.

It's so quick and easy to perk up a pair of plain jeans with stripes of vibrant color that run down the side seam of the legs and around the pockets. Rickrack is inexpensive, comes in lots of colors, and is available from all crafts and notions stores—perfect!

you will need

Rickrack trim, bright pink, about 3¼ yards (3 m) (see Style Solutions, below)
Scissors, embroidery
Sewing needle (see Needles, page 6)
Sewing thread, bright pink

STYLE SOLUTIONS

You can choose a rickrack to complement an existing color accent on your jeans, if there is one. On these jeans the flat fell seams were topstitched in pale pink, so a bright pink rickrack worked well. Alternatively, just choose a rickrack in your favorite color.

1 Cut the end of the rickrack straight through the middle of a scallop. Turn it under behind the next scallop and sew a tiny stitch on either side. Secure the thread (see Securing Threads, page 9) and cut it.

2 Bring the needle and thread from the inside of the jeans to the top of the first stitch on the outside leg seam. Butt the folded end of the rickrack against the bottom of the waistband, above where the needle originally emerged. Slip the needle through a couple of threads on the back of the rickrack and pull the thread through, pulling the rickrack down to the seam stitching.

3 From right to left, slip the needle under the next stitch along the seam.

4 Fold the rickrack back so that the fold is level with the stitch the needle passed under. From left to right, slip the needle through a couple of threads on the back of the rickrack. Gently pull the thread taut. Repeat Steps 3–4 until the entire length of seam is covered with rickrack.

GETTING IT RIGHT

You can slip the needle either left to right or right to left under the stitch, whichever is more comfortable, but you must go through the rickrack in the opposite direction to pull the two elements tightly together. Rickrack is tightly woven from strong fibers, so you need to catch only a couple of strands on the back to hold it firmly against the seam.

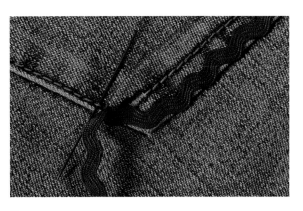

5 Cut the rickrack ¾ inch (2 cm) below the hem of the jeans. Fold the end under the hem and sew it to the back. Secure the thread.

6 Outline the back pockets with rickrack, using the same technique. Rickrack is very flexible and will curve easily around the corners. Fold over the ends as described in Step 1 for a neat finish.

daisy shorts

These shorts look so cute sprinkled with fresh white daisies. Sew the trimming on around the legs (see Attaching Flat Trimmings, page 11), then cut off single flowers and sew them to the front of the shorts with a stitch through each petal.

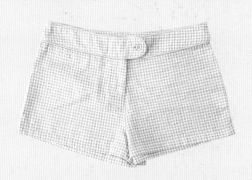

Blue-and-white checked beach shorts.

you will need

- Daisy trimming, white, (see How Much?, below)
- Sewing needle (see Needles, page 6)
- Sewing thread, white
- Scissors, embroidery

HOW MUCH?
You need enough trimming to go around both legs of the shorts, plus about 20 more flowers to decorate the front.

flower tank

A favorite summer top for so many of us, the tank is easy to wear but not very visually exciting. Customize yours with a spray of felt flowers wandering down one shoulder.

Slate blue, V-necked jersey tank with wide shoulder straps.

you will need

Flower motifs (see page 125)

Vanishing fabric marker

Felt fabric, fawn and pale orange, 8¾-inches (22-cm) square, 1 of each

Scissors, embroidery and paper

Small safety pins, 6

Embroidery needle (see Needles, page 6)

Embroidery floss, apple green and pale gold, 1 skein of each

GETTING IT RIGHT

The flowers are small and so can be a little tricky to cut out, but don't worry about their being a perfect shape, as a little irregularity adds to the naïve feel.

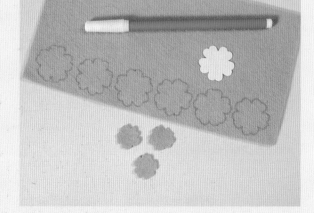

1 Photocopy the motifs and using the paper scissors cut them out to make templates. Draw around the larger flower six times on the fawn felt and the smaller flower six times on the orange felt. Cut out all the felt flowers with the embroidery scissors (see Getting it Right, above right).

2 Arrange the fawn flowers for the best effect on the tank, placing them in an undulating line from high on one shoulder strap down to the central V of the neckline. Slip a safety pin into the tank fabric to mark the position of each flower.

3 Cut a long length of green floss and split it into two three-strand lengths. Thread the embroidery needle with one length and knot one end. Starting on the shoulder strap, work a wavy line of small chain stitch (see page 13) from pin to pin, leaving the pins in place. If you need to start a new length of floss, do so next to a pin where it won't show.

4 Lay an orange flower centrally on a fawn one. Remove a safety pin and lay the double flower in its place.

5 Cut and split a length of gold floss and thread the needle, as in Step 3. Bring the needle from the back of the tank fabric through the center of the flower. Make a straight stitch toward the top edge of an orange petal, taking the needle through the flower and tank fabric. Bring the needle up at the center again and repeat to sew the flower to the tank with five different-length straight stitches, one on each orange petal. Secure the thread on the back. Repeat Steps 4–5 to attach all six flowers.

flower camisole

Pale blue, cotton, camisole top with shoestring straps.

You can buy fabric flower shapes in craft and notions stores, so if cutting out felt flowers doesn't appeal, then go shopping! These lilac velour flowers are store-bought and are ideal on this pretty camisole top.

you will need

- Lilac velour flowers, ¾-inch (2-cm) diameter, 7
- Small safety pins, 6
- Scissors, embroidery
- Embroidery needle (see Needles, page 6)
- Embroidery floss, pale green and pale pink, 1 skein of each

cute puppy t-shirt

This is an almost instant way of making a plain white T-shirt look fab, and if you've stained or marked the front, careful positioning of the photograph can hide the evidence. All you need are a couple of products—no sewing required! Choose a favorite photo and heat up the iron.

White, cotton, long-sleeved T-shirt.

you will need

Photograph printed from a computer onto image transfer paper (see Getting it Right, on page 38)
Scissors, paper
Iron
Iron-on rhinestones
Scrap of cotton fabric

1 Following the instructions on the package of image transfer paper, print out your picture, and cut it out. Lay the picture facedown in position on the T-shirt and iron the back for the required time.

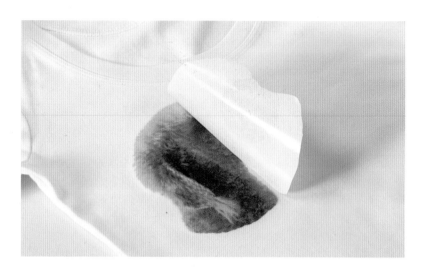

2 Let the transfer paper cool, then carefully peel off the backing.

3 Position the rhinestones for the best effect on the picture. Here they make a collar for the dog. Following the instructions, lay a scrap of fabric over the stones, making sure that the area of the picture the stones are on is covered. Iron the stones for the required time, then remove the fabric. Decorate the neck of the T-shirt with a few more rhinestones for extra sparkle.

love
t-shirt

This T-shirt is decorated in the same way as the Cute Puppy T-shirt, but using a computer-generated image. You'll find the image at the back of this book, so you can scan it into your computer or use a piece of freeware art downloaded from an Internet site. To find images, simply type in the name of the subject you are searching for into your favorite search engine.

White, cotton, short-sleeved T-shirt.

you will need

Winged heart motif (see page 125) printed from a computer onto image transfer paper
Scissors, paper
Iron
Iron-on rhinestone heart motif
Scrap of cotton fabric

pink jewel
sweater

This is a flattering style of sweater, but the neckline can be rather severe if the sweater is a solid color. Soften the shape of the neck and lift the color by adding a knitted trim to the neckline in a paler shade of the same color. Sew-on gems add extra color and sparkly detail.

Hot pink, fine machine-knit sweater with faux wrapover neckline.

you will need

Knitted trimming with selvedge, pale pink (see How Much?, below)

Pins

Sewing needle (see Needles, page 6)

Sewing thread, hot pink

Scissors, embroidery

Sew-on gems, pink and lilac colors, 2 circular, 10 teardrop (1 pink and 1 lilac circular; 5 pink and 5 lilac teardrop)

HOW MUCH?

You will need enough trimming to go around the neckline from the waist at one side to the V in the center plus ½ inch (1 cm).

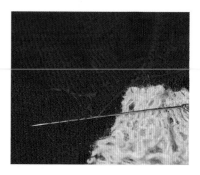

1 Starting at the waist, pin the trimming to the faux wrapover neckline with the ruffled edge standing upright and the selvedge edge inside the neckline. Using the needle and thread, sew the bottom edge of the selvedge around the neckline (see Attaching Trimmings to Knitted Fabric, page 11). Remove pins.

3 Using the needle and doubled thread, sew a circular gem to the front of the sweater. Place it close to the neckline to the right of the central V, and make three or four stitches through each of the holes in the gem.

5 To avoid loops of thread when moving from one end of a petal to the other, slip the needle through the back of some stitches in the knitted fabric.

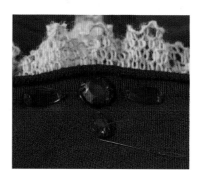

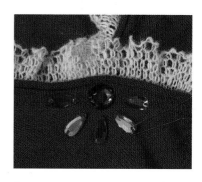

2 At the central V in the neckline, turn the trimming ½ inch (1 cm) under in a tiny double hem and sew in place. (If your trimming frays easily, make a similar hem at the waist when you start sewing.)

4 Using the same method, sew one petal either side of the gem at the edge of the neckline, and one between them.

6 Sew on two more petals, spacing them between the three existing ones. Repeat Steps 3–6 to make another gem "flower" close to the shoulder on the same side of the sweater.

STYLE SOLUTIONS

Sew-on gems are available in a variety of shapes, so choose ones to suit your sweater— a trail of sparkly hearts maybe? Be careful not to sew on too many gems or their weight may drag on the neckline and pull the fine knitted fabric out of shape.

buttons
and beads

pearl button vest

Heart buttons with hanging bead strands, squares crossed with lines of beads, flowers with beaded stamens, circles and ovals with bead dots—pick out the detail on a vest with strips of pearl buttons attached using these different techniques. They are all easy and quick to work, so you can transform your vest in just a couple of hours.

Striped wool vest with lapels.

Mother-of-pearl buttons, selection of different shapes and sizes (see How Much?, below)
Seed beads, size 12, blue glass lined in pink, about 425
Beading needle, size 13
Beading thread, size D, pale blue
Scissors, embroidery
Mother-of-pearl buttons, same size to replace existing closure buttons

HOW MUCH?

Five differently shaped buttons were used on this vest: circles, ovals, squares, hearts, and flowers, all with two holes in them. In total, 44 buttons were used.

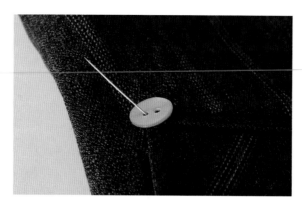

1 To attach a circular or oval button, thread the beading needle and knot one end of the thread. Lay the button in position (see Style Solutions, right), and bring the needle up from the back of the vest through a buttonhole.

STYLE SOLUTIONS

Use the buttons to pick out areas of detail on your vest. Here, the buttons follow a stripe down each lapel. Trim all the pocket welts and add brooch-like detail on one side of the collar. Make the arrangements asymmetrical to add interest to the design.

2 Pick up a bead, then return the needle down through the same buttonhole. Repeat for the other buttonhole. Secure the thread on the fabric back (see Securing Threads, page 9).

4 Pick up two more beads, take the needle through the two beads on the button, then pick up two more beads. Take the needle down through the fabric on the other side of the button. The line of beads can run horizontally or vertically. Secure the thread on the fabric back.

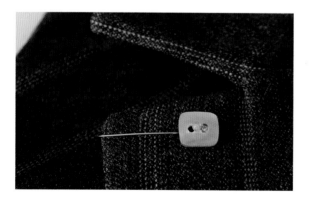

3 To attach a square button, follow Step 1. Pick up two beads and take the needle down through the other buttonhole. Bring the needle out through the fabric at one side of the button and in line with the holes.

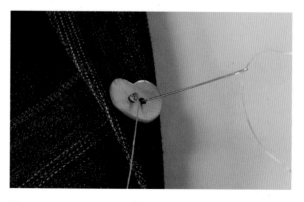

5 To attach a heart button, follow Step 1. Pick up three beads, then take the needle down through the other buttonhole.

6 Bring the needle up through the first buttonhole and the first bead. Pick up 15 to 20 beads.

7 Skipping the last bead, return the needle back through the string of beads and through the central bead on the button. Pull gently on the thread to pull the beads up close to those on the button.

8 Pick up 10 to 15 beads, then repeat Step 7, but this time take the needle through the last bead on the button, then through the hole. Secure the thread on the fabric back.

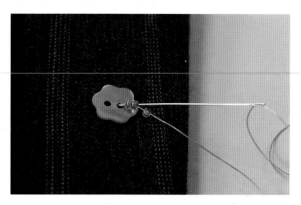

9 To attach a flower button, follow Step 1. Pick up three beads, then skipping the last bead take the needle back down through the beads and same buttonhole. Repeat for the other buttonhole. Secure the thread on the fabric back.

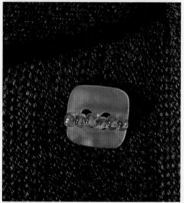

10 Remove original buttons, fastening the vest closed. Repeat Step 1, positioning a new button where an original one was positioned. Pick up enough beads to span the gap between the holes, then take the needle down through the other hole. Take the needle through the holes and beads several more times to attach the button securely. Repeat for all original buttons.

GETTING IT RIGHT

As the decorative buttons will not be subject to much wear and tear, and the beading thread is quite strong, attaching them with just one stitch is fine. However, it is a good idea to secure the thread after attaching each button. This way, if one button does come unfastened, you won't lose any more.

vintage button
trousers

Here's the excuse you've been looking for to raid Grandma's button box and make good use of the treasures you find. Keep the look stylish by sticking to a simple color palette— brown and pink buttons complement the color of these trousers beautifully. Decoratively arrange the buttons to the best advantage on the trouser cuffs and pockets, putting the choicest finds where they'll attract most attention.

you will need

- Vintage buttons, as many as you can beg, borrow, or steal!
- Sewing needle (see Needles, page 6)
- Sewing thread, fawn
- Scissors, embroidery

Fawn, jumbo-cord, three-quarter-length trousers with deep cuffs.

toggled cargo shorts

Replacing boring or plain buttons with something more interesting is a very quick and easy way of adding an original touch to a garment. These street-style cargo shorts have had their plastic buttons swapped for wooden toggles attached with knotted leather thongs. Use the same technique to replace the buttons on a denim or corduroy jacket.

Below-the-knee, khaki shorts with button-down cargo pockets and buttoned cuffs.

you will need

- Leather thong, pale tan, 10 inches (25 cm) per button
- Sewing needle (see Needles, page 6)
- Sewing thread, pale tan
- Scissors
- Wooden toggles, one per button (see Getting it Right, page 53)
- Pins

1 Remove the original buttons and mark the button positions with pins. Thread the needle with a long length of thread, double it and knot the ends together. Fold a length of leather thong in half and pinch it to mark the center. Lay this point on the marking pin and sew a few stitches over it to hold it securely in place. Secure the thread on the fabric back (see Securing Threads, page 9). Remove pin.

3 Thread each end of the thong through a hole in a toggle.

2 Tie a firm single knot in the thong, covering the stitches.

4 Push the toggle up toward the single knot. Tie the ends of the thong in an overhand knot and pull it tight so that it sits about 1 inch (2.5 cm) below the toggle. Repeat Steps 1–4 to replace all the buttons with wooden toggles.

GETTING IT RIGHT

Wooden toggles are available in various shapes and sizes, so bear the following in mind when choosing toggles for your own garment. Look for toggles with two holes in them, rather than the type with a groove running around the middle. The holes must be large enough for the leather thong to pass through. The toggles must fit through the buttonholes, but as the leather thong allows them to hang loosely from the fabric they can be turned to button them up, so they can be quite a tight fit. If in doubt, buy one toggle and attach it to check that it goes through the buttonhole before buying the rest.

beaded flower blouse

White, crinkled-cotton blouse with machine-embroidered flower pattern in pink and lilac.

Machine embroidery is a popular decorative feature on even the most inexpensive clothing, but it can be made more decorative by adding some sparkling Delica beads. This may look painstaking, but it's a surprisingly quick technique to work. The pattern and color choices are dictated by the blouse's existing embroidery—a sewer's version of paint-by-numbers. This blouse has an allover floral design and I've chosen to bead just the flower heads. If you like the effect but don't want to do so much beading, then turn to Another Idea, page 56.

you will need

Beading needle, size 13
Beading thread, size D, white
Scissors, embroidery
Delica beads, pink and lilac (see How Much?, below)
Flat sequins, ¼-inch (6-mm) diameter, bright pink and rose pink (see How Much?, below)

HOW MUCH?

As the quantities of beads and sequins you will need depends entirely on the pattern of your shirt and how much beading you want to do, it's impossible to give specific quantities. However, there are a couple of ways of estimating quantities. Review the garment, decide which areas of the pattern you want to bead, and count the stitches in just one of the areas. Multiply this by the number of areas and you have a rough quantity (though do buy more than you think you need, just in case). If this sounds like hard work, or you can't decide on a beading pattern, just buy a big bag of beads; they aren't terribly expensive.

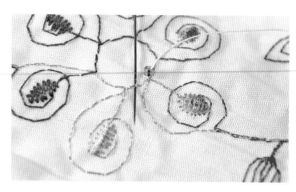

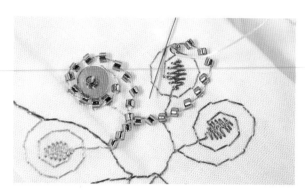

1 Thread the needle with a long length of thread and knot one end. Bring the needle from the back of the shirt fabric between two of the machine-embroidered stitches. Pick up a bead, then slip the needle under the next machine-embroidered stitch.

3 Repeat Steps 2–3 to cover all the stitches in the selected area with beads. Change bead color to reflect the color change in the embroidery. At the end of a line of beading, return the needle through to the back of the fabric.

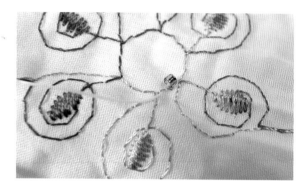

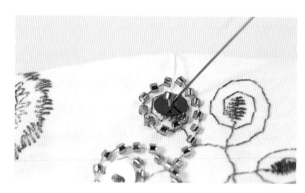

2 Pull the thread through so that the bead lies at a slight angle on top of the stitch.

4 To attach sequins, bring the needle from the back of the fabric to the position of the sequin. Pick up a sequin and matching-color bead. Return the needle back down through the sequin and fabric at the same place it came out. Pull the thread tight and make a tiny securing stitch through the fabric behind the sequin. To avoid loops of thread when moving from one beaded area to another on the back of the fabric, slip the needle through the backs of the machine-embroidered stitches.

Another idea

If you like the beaded finish but are short on time, you can just bead a single motif, as shown here. The visual effect is of a perfectly coordinated brooch. Alternatively, bead just a specific area of the garment—a pocket or cuff, for instance.

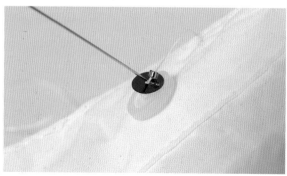

5 To top each button with a sequin, bring the needle up through the fabric and one of the buttonholes. Pick up a sequin and bead. Return the needle through the sequin and the other buttonhole and through the fabric. Pull the thread tight and secure it on the back of the fabric (see Securing Threads, page 9).

stripy
beaded scarf

This scarf is stitched with beads carefully chosen to highlight some of the stripe colors. Beading knitted fabric is easy as the stitches and rows form a grid you can follow, but the thread stops the fabric stretching, so don't bead a cuff you need to stretch to get on. The beads are sewn on with backstitch, one bead for each stitch.

Fine yarn, machine-knitted, striped wool scarf.

you will need

- Beading needle, size 13
- Beading threads, size D, pale pink, orange, apple green, and pale blue
- Scissors, embroidery
- Matte seed beads, size 12 pale pink, orange, and aqua
- Satin-finish bugle beads, ¼-inch (6-mm) long, apple green and pale blue

sparkle sequin bolero jacket

Sequins add instant glamour, and these large ones cover the fabric quickly. The bow fastening is so fashionable, but bows can be difficult to tie perfectly. Instead of spending ages in front of the mirror trying to get it right, cheat by making this permanent bow that always looks fantastic.

Burgundy, short-sleeved, chenille bolero jacket with mandarin collar and edge-to-edge front fastening.

you will need

Cup sequins, ½-inch (12-mm) diameter, bright bronze, about 100

Flat sequins, ¼-inch (6-mm) diameter, dark bronze, about 100

Seed beads, size 10, bronze, about 100

Beading needle, size 13

Beading thread, size D, burgundy

Scissors, embroidery

Double-sided satin ribbon, 1⅜-inches (3.5-cm) wide, dark brown, 15 inches (37 cm), 1 piece; 18 inches (45 cm), 1 piece; 3¼ inches (8 cm), 1 piece

Sewing needle (see Needles, page 6)

Sewing thread, dark brown

Snap fastener, 1, 7-mm diameter

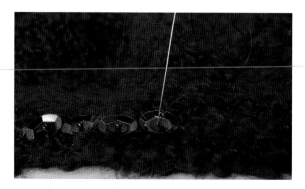

1 Thread the beading needle with a long length of beading thread and knot one end. Lay a cup sequin in position on the bolero collar and bring the needle up through the central hole. Pick up a flat sequin and then a seed bead. Return the needle back down through the sequins and fabric at the same place it came out.

4 Place the crease made in Step 3 along the row of stitching, making an equal-sized ribbon loop on each side. Stitch another line of small running stitches over the first line, stitching through all the ribbon layers. Gather up the running stitches tightly and secure the thread. This makes the looped part of the bow.

2 Repeat Step 1 to cover the collar with rows of sequins. Place the sequins close together and stagger alternate rows.

5 Crease the 18-inch (45-cm) long piece of ribbon in the middle. Using the needle and thread as before, work a line of running stitches along the crease. Pull up the thread tightly to gather and secure the thread. This makes the tails of the bow. Using the needle and doubled thread, sew the tails to the back of the gathered area of the bow loops.

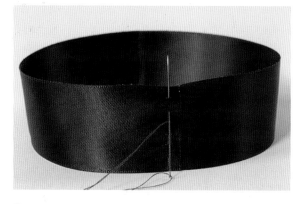

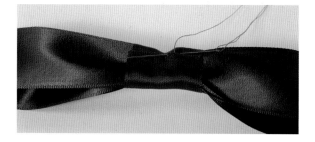

3 Fold the 15-inch (37-cm) long piece of ribbon in half and mark the middle with a crease. Overlap the cut ends of the ribbon by ½ inch (1 cm). Thread the sewing needle with brown thread, double it, and knot the ends. Hand-sew a line of small running stitches along the middle of the overlap to form a ribbon circle. Secure the thread with a couple of backstitches (see Securing Threads, page 9).

6 Fold over and crease ½ inch (1 cm) at one end of the 3¼-inch (8-cm) long piece of ribbon. Wrap this ribbon around the joined gathers with the folded end overlapping the raw end at the back. Ensure that this ribbon is placed quite tightly around the gathers. Using the sewing needle and single thread, sew the folded end in place.

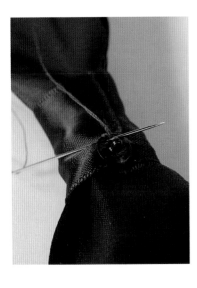

7 Sew half of the snap fastener to one edge of the central section of the bow.

8 Tack the other side of the central ribbon to one side of the collar, making sure that the bow is positioned centrally on the front of the bolero.

9 Making sure that the bow is lying straight, sew the other half of the snap fastener to the other side of the collar, aligning it with the first half of the fastener.

beaded miniskirt

Beading isn't difficult, but it does take a little time, so this flexible project is an ideal introduction to the craft. You can start with just a few flowers, wear the skirt, then add more flowers as the impulse takes you. You can work the same flower designs on almost any garment—just scatter them to suit the garment's shape and your own taste.

Unlined, gray, needle cord, pleated miniskirt.

you will need

Beading needle, size 13
Beading thread, size D, pale gray
Scissors, embroidery
Seed beads, size 12, silver (see How Much?, below)
Bugle beads, 1/4-inch (6-mm) long, silver (see How Much?, below)
Sequins, 1/8-inch (2-mm) diameter, silver (see How Much?, below)

HOW MUCH?

As the quantity of beads needed depends entirely on how much beading you want to do, it's impossible to give precise quantities. As a guide, the first flower uses eight seed beads and one sequin; the second, one seed bead and seven sequins; the third, 101 seed beads and one sequin; and the fourth 25 seed beads and ten bugle beads. The beading shown on this skirt used a total of 423 seed beads, 20 bugle beads and 53 sequins.

GETTING IT RIGHT

As the beading thread will show on the sequins, choose a thread color that closely matches them. If you find it impossible to get a good match, use a matching sewing thread and a slim sewing needle to sew on the sequins.

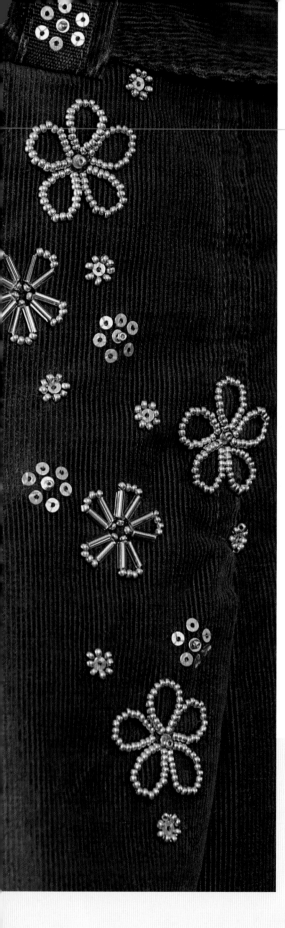

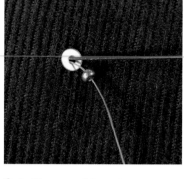

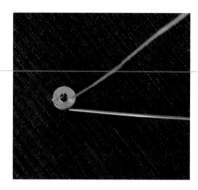

1 To work the smallest flower, place a sequin on the fabric for the flower center. Bring the needle from the back of the fabric through the hole of the sequin and make a straight stitch over the sequin, taking the needle back down next to the sequin's outer edge. Repeat twice more, spacing the stitches evenly around the sequin.

3 A different small flower is made by bringing the needle up through the fabric and threading on a sequin and a seed bead. Take the needle down through the sequin and fabric to make the flower center.

2 Bring the needle from the back of the fabric close to the edge of the sequin and pick up a bead. Return the needle close to where it came out. Pull gently so that the bead lies on its side. Sew on seven more beads. To space the beads evenly around the sequin, sew on a bead at each point of the compass, then sew a bead between each of these. Secure the thread on the back (see Securing Threads, page 9).

4 Following Step 1, stitch six sequins around the flower center, positioning them close to, but not touching the center sequin. To space them evenly, sew one on either side of the center, then sew on two more between them. Secure the thread on the back.

5 To make a large daisy, thread the beading needle with a 2¼-yards (2-m) length of thread, double it, and knot the ends together (see Getting it Right, right). Following Step 3, make a flower center. Bring the needle up next to the sequin and pick up 20 seed beads.

GETTING IT RIGHT

When working with a long length of thread that is doubled, pull it slowly through the beads or it will tend to tangle and knot. When working the bead embroidery, be careful not to catch any pocket linings or the backs of pleats with the stitching. If you do, you won't be able to use the pockets and the pleats may hang oddly.

8 Spread the loops out flat on the fabric to form a pretty flower shape. Sew a tiny tacking stitch over the end of each loop, between the tenth and eleventh beads, to hold the loop in place. Secure the thread on the back.

6 Push the needle to the back next to where it came up originally and pull the thread gently to form a loop. If your beads are reluctant to form a smooth loop, bring the needle back up again at the starting point and take the thread through all the beads once or twice more. Return the needle through the fabric—the thicker bulk of thread will encourage the beads to sit smoothly next to one another.

7 Bring the needle up to make the second petal and pick up another 20 beads. Repeat this around the flower center to make five evenly spaced loops.

9 To make a star daisy, bring the needle up through the fabric. Pick up a seed bead, a bugle bead, four seed beads, and another bugle bead. Take the needle through the first seed bead and back down. To form a petal shape, bring the needle up at the starting point and back through the beads. Make five petals. Repeat Step 8, making the tacking stitch between the second and third seed beads, to complete the star.

Left and opposite page: Use your imagination to create a range of pretty flowers.

fluffy feathers sweater

Cashmere/wool blend, turquoise, short-sleeved sweater.

This fabulously extravagant feather corsage with a glittering sequin and bead center will turn the plainest garment into a party piece. It's shown here on a short-sleeved sweater for a retro look, but it'll work just as well on a jacket or dress.

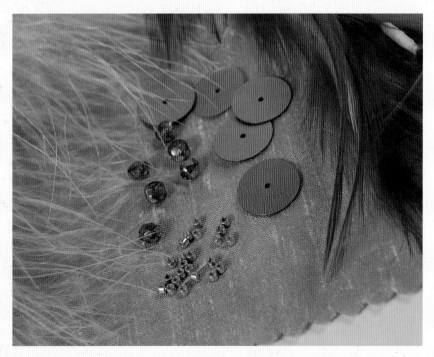

you will need

Metal self-cover button, 1¼-inches (29-mm) diameter, 1 half dome

Silk fabric, lilac, 3¼-inches (8-cm) square, 1 piece

Vanishing fabric marker

Felt, lilac, 2-inches (5-cm) square, 1 piece

Scissors, embroidery

Beading needle, size 13

Beading thread, size D, purple

Flat sequins, ½-inch (12-mm) diameter, mauve, 9

Fire-polished beads, 4 mm, pink, 9

Delica beads, lilac, 9

Marabou feathers, lilac, 6

Feather plumes, mauve, 6

Fabric glue

Sewing needle (see Needles, page 6)

Sewing thread, turquoise

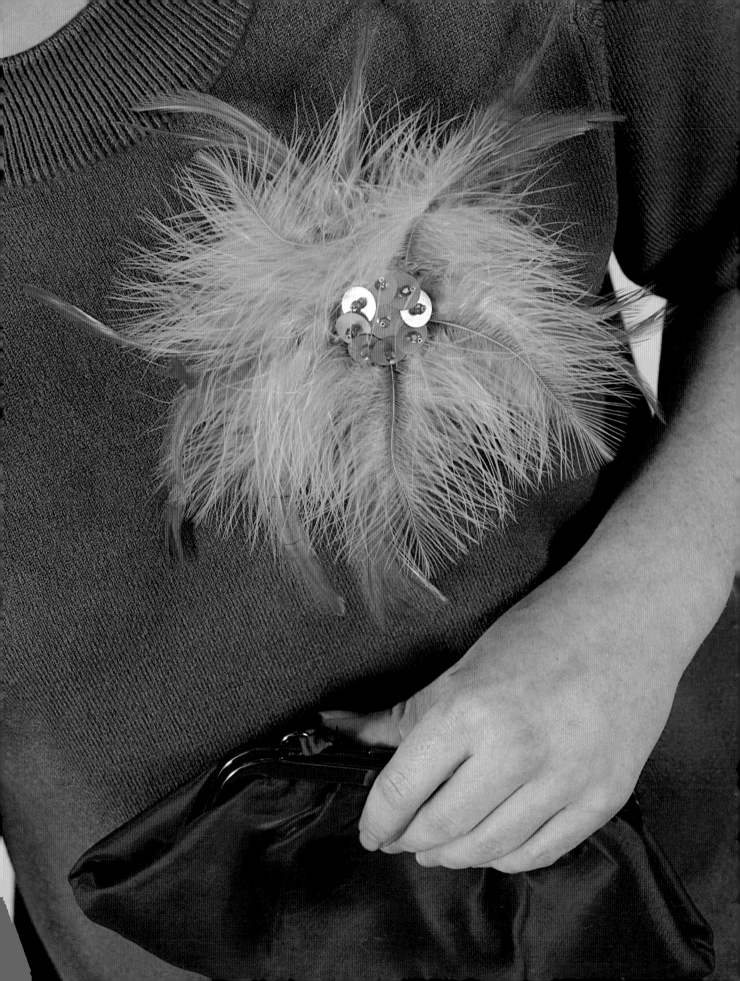

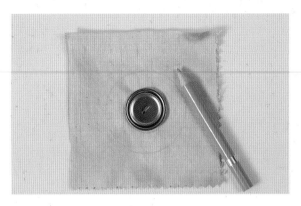

1 Lay the template from the button kit on the silk and draw around it with the fabric marker. Lay the back of the button in the center of this circle and draw around that, too.

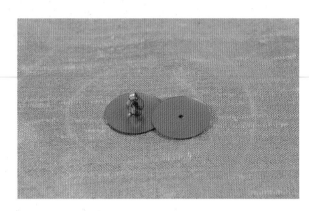

4 Lay another sequin on the fabric with one edge overlapping the inner drawn circle and the other overlapping the central sequin. Bring the needle up through the hole and pick up the beads and attach the sequin as in Step 2.

2 Draw around the button back onto the felt. Cut out the circle just inside the drawn line. Set this aside.

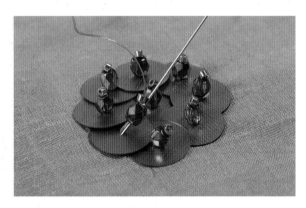

5 Repeat to form a ring of eight overlapping sequins. Tuck the edge of the last sequin under the edge of the first one to make the ring continuous. Remove any visible marks from the inner circle.

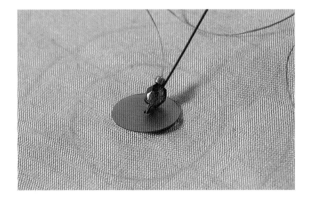

3 Thread the beading needle with a long length of beading thread and knot one end. Lay a sequin in the center of the silk circle and bring the needle from the back of the fabric through the sequin's hole. Pick up a fire-polished bead and then a Delica bead. Return the needle back down through the fire-polished bead, the sequin, and the fabric.

6 Following the instructions in the button kit, cover the button with the sequin-decorated fabric.

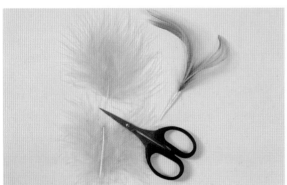

7 Cut the marabou feathers to about 3 inches (8 cm) long, using the embroidery scissors. Cut the feather plumes down to 4 inches (10 cm) long.

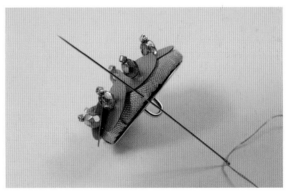

8 Thread the beading needle with a long length of beading thread and knot one end. Take the needle through the fabric on the back edge of the covered button and pull it through.

9 Lay a marabou feather against the back of the button, next to the thread. Bring the needle back between the barbs of the feather, around the quill, between the barbs on the other side, and through the edge of the fabric again, close to the first stitch. Pull the thread tight. Make a few more stitches over the first one in the same way. Secure the thread in the fabric on the edge of the button (see Securing Threads, page 9).

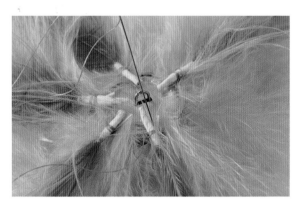

10 Repeat Steps 8–9 to attach the remaining marabou feathers to the button, spacing them evenly around the edge. Attach the plume feathers in the same way, stitching over the stitches holding the marabou feathers to the button.

12 Using the sewing needle and doubled thread, sew the corsage to the front of the sweater with a few stitches through the button shank. To launder the sweater, just snip the stitches, and then later reattach the corsage.

STYLE SOLUTIONS

Make a coordinated piece of jewelry by using a smaller button and sequins and shorter feathers and sew it to a ribbon to make a choker or wrist corsage.

11 Using the embroidery scissors, cut a tiny slot in the center of the felt circle to fit over the button shank. Glue the felt circle to the back of the decorated button, using the fabric glue.

ribbons

silky ribbon shirt

Shimmering fabrics and vibrant color combine in this project to produce a sophisticated, glamorous shirt that you can wear to the chicest party with confidence. No one will ever guess that you had a hand in making it.

Turquoise, silky shirt with concealed buttonhole band.

STYLE SOLUTIONS

The look of this project is very dependent on the right mix of colors; you need a fairly simple, strong color palette. Take your garment with you when shopping for the ribbon and sequins, and make sure that you look at the colors in good natural light, not artificial light—you'll be amazed at how different colors can look. Be brave with the combinations: try tangerine ribbon on a brown shirt, with pale orange sequins and beads; or lilac ribbon on a pink shirt with violet sequins and beads.

you will need

Satin ribbon, 1-inch (2.5-cm) wide, chartreuse green, (see How Much?, below)

Pins

Sewing needle, (see Needles, page 6)

Scissors, embroidery

Sewing machine

Sewing threads, chartreuse green and cream

Beading needle, size 13

Beading thread, size D, chartreuse green

Square sequins, ⅜ inch (1 cm) across, pale green, about 20

Delica beads, pale green, about 8

Pins

HOW MUCH?

You will need two pieces of satin ribbon, each the length of the front of the shirt, from neckband to hem, plus 1¼ inches (3 cm).

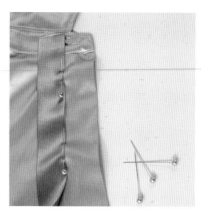

1 Pin a length of ribbon to the right front of the shirt with the front edge just covering the line of stitching at the edge of the buttonhole band welt, and ½ inch (1 cm) standing above the bottom of the neckband.

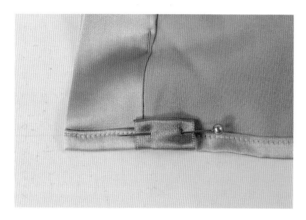

2 At the shirt hem, fold under ½ inch (1 cm) of ribbon, then fold the remainder under the hem and pin it in place.

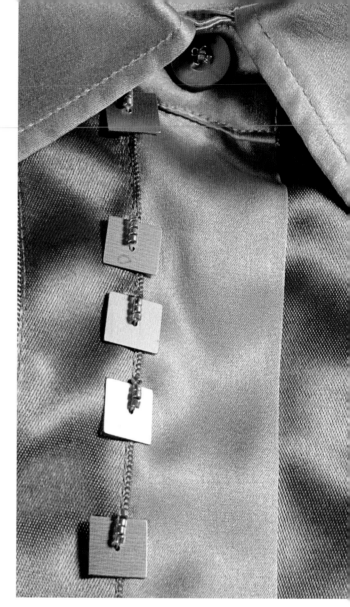

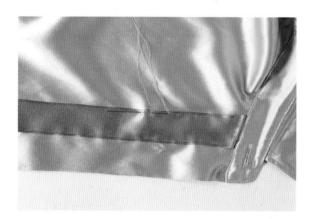

3 At the neck, fold under the end of the ribbon so that the folded edge aligns with the bottom edge of the neckband. Baste across the top folded edge and down each long edge with the cream thread, removing the pins as you stitch.

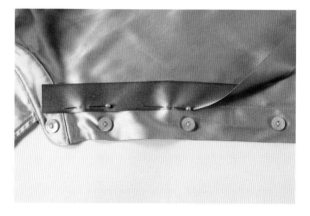

4 Following Steps 1–3, pin and baste the other piece of ribbon to the button band with the front edge of the ribbon just covering the line of stitching.

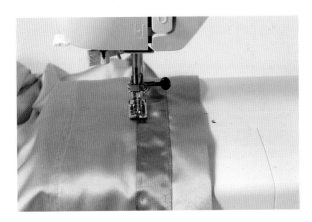

5 Thread the sewing machine with the green thread and set it to a medium straight stitch. Machine stitch the ribbon to the shirt (see Attaching Ribbon, page 12). Remove the basting threads.

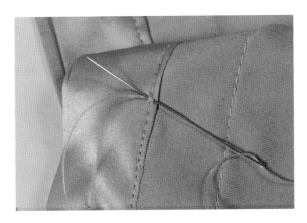

7 Sew a tiny securing stitch in the fabric beneath the ribbon, then slip the needle between the ribbon and shirt fabric to emerge at the next sequin position. Sew on about 20 sequins spaced randomly along the edge of the ribbon. Secure the thread on the back, when you have finished sewing on all the sequins (see Securing Threads, page 9).

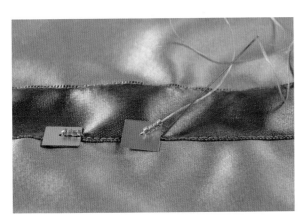

6 Thread the beading needle with a long length of beading thread and knot one end. Place a sequin in position on the edge of the ribbon decorating the buttonhole band and near the neckband. Bring the needle from the back of the fabric through the hole in the sequin. Pick up four Delica beads (or as many as is needed to span the sequin from hole to edge). Return the needle back down through the fabric at the top edge of the sequin.

8 To decorate the visible top button, bring the needle from the back through the fabric and one buttonhole and pick up a Delica bead. Take the needle under the thread between the buttonholes. Repeat until the center of the button is filled with beads. Then take the needle down through the other buttonhole and secure the thread on the back of the fabric.

ruched skirt

Color-matching ribbons and a touch of lace spice up a tartan winter skirt. Wear it during the day with long boots and a jacket, or dress it up with high heels for an evening out.

Burnt orange, maroon, and cream tartan, lined A-line skirt in soft wool fabric.

you will need

- Sewing needle (see Needles, page 6)
- Sewing threads, maroon and burnt orange
- Satin ribbon, 1-inch (2.5-cm) wide, wine-red, 9½ inches (24 cm), 1 piece
- Grosgrain ribbon, ⅝-inch (1.5-cm) wide, burnt orange, 9½ inches (24 cm), 1 piece
- Pins
- Sewing machine
- Scissors, embroidery
- Decorative button, ⅝-inch (1.5-cm) diameter, dark brown
- Lace, 7-inches (18-cm) deep, maroon, 16 inches (40 cm), 1 piece

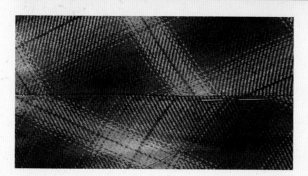

1 Thread the needle with the maroon thread, double it, and knot the ends. Handstitch an 8-inch (20-cm) long line of running stitches ¼ inch (0.5 cm) on either side of one side seam. Make the stitches about ½ inch (1 cm) long and sew the two rows so that the stitches are aligned. Start at the hem edge and finish with the threads on the back of the fabric. Do not catch the skirt lining with the stitches.

2 On the wrong side, pull up the threads tightly so the gathered section is 1½ inches (4 cm) deep. Knot the threads securely together on the inside of the skirt to hold the gathers, then secure them into the seam allowance (see Securing Threads, page 9).

3 Center and pin the narrow ribbon on top of the wide ribbon. Set the sewing machine to a medium straight stitch and, using orange thread, sew the ribbons together along both edges of the narrow ribbon (see Attaching Ribbon, page 12). Remove pins.

4 Set the sewing machine to a tight zigzag stitch and sew across both ends of the ribbons to neaten them and to keep them from fraying.

5 Fold over 1¼ inches (3 cm) of ribbon at one end to make a loop. Set the sewing machine to a small straight stitch and machine stitch across the narrow ribbon at the bottom of the loop. Secure the threads on the back.

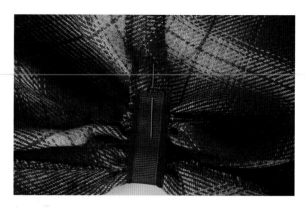

8 Position the other end of the ribbon under the skirt hem and adjust it so that it sits snugly over the ruching. Stitch this ribbon end to the seam allowance on the inside of the skirt, whip stitching over the end.

6 Make a second loop on top of and ½ inch (1 cm) smaller than the first loop. Machine stitch across the bottom as in Step 5, sewing over the same line of stitching.

9 Pin the lace to the lining so that it shows under the ruched section of the skirt. The bottom edge of the lace should hang just below the hem of the lining.

STYLE SOLUTIONS

If your skirt has any existing buttons, replace them with decorative buttons to match the one on the ribbon loop for a coordinated finish.

7 Pin the loops to the skirt with the line of stitching just above the ruched section and centered on the side seam. Place the button on the line of stitching and, using burnt orange thread, sew it through the ribbons and to the skirt fabric. Remove pins.

10 Set the sewing machine to a medium straight stitch and machine stitch across the top edge and down each side of the lace to hold it in position. Remove pins.

ruched-sleeve tunic blouse

Use the same ruching technique to trim sleeves with no cuffs. Here, the visible front of the suedette ribbon (suedette is a fake suede fabric) is edged with beads (see Beaded Blanket Stitch, page 14), and the top edge is hand sewn to the top of the ruched section of the sleeve with tiny stitches through the beads.

Bright red, linen tunic blouse with long sleeves without cuffs.

glamorous party skirt

A-line, silk skirt with waistband and side zipper fastening.

As well as being simply stunning, this project is also practical. You spill a drink on your favorite party skirt and the mark won't come out? Make this tulle and ribbon overskirt, and you've got a completely new skirt with no stain visible.

you will need

- Tulle fabric, black (see How Much?, below)
- Pins
- Tape measure
- Scissors, dressmaker's
- Sewing machine
- Sewing thread, black
- Organza ribbon, 1-inch (2.5-cm wide), black, about 5½ yards (5 m)
- Organza ribbon, ¼-inch (5-mm wide), black, about 5½ yards (5 m)
- Grosgrain ribbon, black, (see Getting it Right, page 83)

HOW MUCH?

Lay your skirt flat and measure across the widest point of the hem. You need twice this length of tulle, by the depth of the skirt from waistband to hem, plus ¾ inch (2 cm). If you are not able to use the tulle from selvedge to selvedge for the length of the skirt, buy tulle twice the length of the skirt plus 2 inches (5 cm).

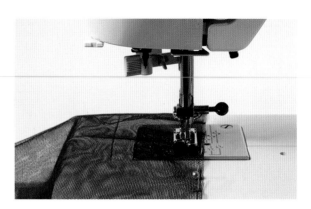

1 Trim the cut edges straight and cut off both selvedge edges. Fold the tulle in half with the one selvedge at the top and one at the bottom and lay it flat on a work surface. (If you don't have a surface large enough to lay out the whole piece, then work on the floor.) Center the skirt flat on the tulle with the top of the waistband at one trimmed-off selvedge edge and with ¾ inch (2 cm) of tulle showing below the hem. Pin the layers together, pinning at frequent intervals. Measure out ¾ inch (2 cm) from the hem and put a pin in the tulle. Continue measuring and marking with pins ¾ inch (2 cm) from the hem. Measure out ⅝ inch (1.5 cm) from one side of the skirt and place a pin. Continue measuring and marking with a pin ⅝ inch (1.5 cm) along the side of the skirt. Pin at frequent intervals and in a straight line. Repeat for the other side of the skirt.

3 Thread the sewing machine and set it to a medium straight stitch. Using a ½-inch (1-cm) seam allowance, sew the two layers of tulle together along the side pinned edges. Remove the pins as you sew. On the zipper side, stitch from the marked point to the hem. Trim the seam allowances to ¼ inch (5 mm). Press seams open, pressing under the allowances either side of the unstitched section at the same time.

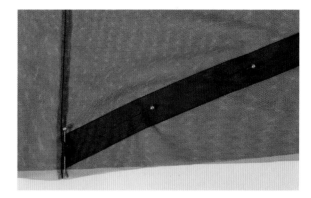

2 Cut the tulle from pin to pin, cutting just outside the pins. Put a pin in the tulle to mark the bottom of the skirt zipper. Remove the pins holding the skirt to the tulle and set the skirt aside.

4 Cut one end of the wide organza ribbon at an angle, fold it under ⅜ inch (1 cm), and pin it to a side seam close to the bottom of the tulle skirt. Continue pinning the ribbon around the tulle (see Style Solutions, below) until you reach the waist.

STYLE SOLUTIONS

You can use the ribbons to make all sorts of different patterns on the tulle. Here, they spiral unevenly around the skirt, from the hem up to the waist, crossing over one another as they spiral. However, you can sew the ribbons on in straight or diagonal lines, in small sections—whatever suits your taste. Pin the overskirt temporarily to the skirt (see Step 7) once you have pinned all the ribbons in place and get an obliging friend to try it on so that you can check the effect. Change ribbon placement, if necessary.

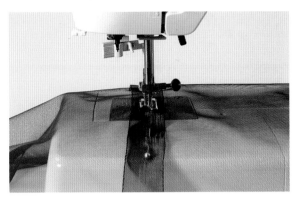

5 Machine stitch the ribbon to the tulle with a single stitching line down the center.

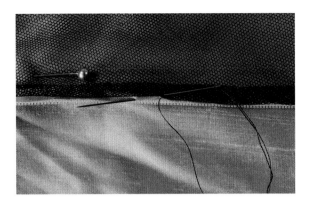

8 Using the sewing needle and black thread, slip stitch the pressed-under edges of the tulle to the edges of the zipper welts.

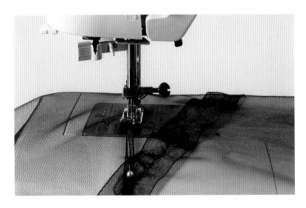

6 Repeat Steps 4–5 with the narrow organza ribbon.

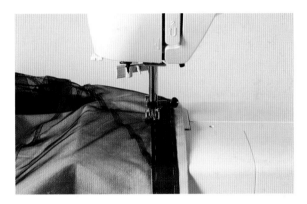

9 Pin, then baste the grosgrain ribbon to the waistband with the bottom edge aligned with the bottom of the waistband (see Getting it Right, below). Remove pins. Machine stitch the ribbon in place (see Attaching Ribbon, page 12).

7 Slip the tulle overskirt over the silk skirt, matching the top edges and side seams. Turn under ½ inch (1 cm) around the top of tulle overskirt; pin, then baste it to the waistband. Remove pins.

GETTING IT RIGHT

The style and width of your skirt waistband affects how you'll attach the ribbon to it and the width and quantity of ribbon needed. This skirt has a 1¼-inch (3-cm) deep waistband and a 1⅜-inches (3.5-cm) long tab extending across the top of the zipper for the snap fastener. I wanted to keep a stripe of the original skirt color visible at the top of the waistband, so I chose a ¾-inch (2-cm) wide ribbon, but you can use one the same width as the waistband, if you prefer. I needed enough ribbon to go around the waistband (including the tab), with an extra ½ inch (1 cm) to fold under the untabbed end, and an extra 1½ inches (4 cm) to fold under the tab. Follow this model when buying ribbon for your own waistband.

velvet jacket

This jacket purchased from a chain-store is a lovely purple color but is otherwise completely plain. Adding the paler, pleated-ribbon cuffs softens the look and emphasizes the rich color. The ribbon and diamanté lapel brooch uses the same ribbon to unite it with the cuffs.

Purple velvet jacket with lapels and plain, straight cuffs.

GETTING IT RIGHT

Measure the circumference of the jacket cuff. Draw a line on a piece of paper the measured length. Divide this measurement into 13 equal lengths. Starting from one end, mark the lengths on the drawn line. There will be a pleat at each marked point. Each pleat is the length of the space between two marked points plus $3/8$ inch (1 cm), so twice that amount of ribbon is needed to make each pleat. The total length of ribbon needed for each cuff is the total amount of all the spaces and pleats added together, plus $3/8$ inch (1 cm) at each end for the seam allowances.

On this jacket, the cuff measures $10^{1}/_4$ inches (26 cm) around. There are 13 spaces between pleats with each space measuring $3/4$ inch (2 cm). Each pleat is $1^{1}/_8$ inches (3 cm) deep, so $2^{1}/_4$ inches (6 cm) of ribbon is needed for each one. Therefore the total amount of ribbon needed is:

13 x $3/4$ inch (2 cm) for the spaces = $10^{1}/_4$ inches (26 cm)

13 x $2^{1}/_4$ inches (6 cm) for the pleats = $29^{1}/_4$ inches (78 cm)

2 x $1/4$ inch (1 cm) for the seam allowances = $3/4$ inch (2 cm)

Ribbon needed for each cuff = $41^{3}/_4$ inches (106 cm)

PLEATED VELVET CUFFS

Velvet ribbon, 2-inches (5-cm) wide, lilac (see How Much?, below)
Tape measure
Chalk fabric marker
Pins
Sewing needle (see Needles, page 6)
Scissors, embroidery
Sewing machine
Sewing thread, lilac, and cream

HOW MUCH?

To work out how much ribbon you will need to make pleated cuffs for your own jacket, follow the instructions carefully and refer to the diagram on page 125. It may sound like a complicated calculation, but it really isn't.

1 Cut each end of a length of ribbon straight. Lay it face down and measure ³⁄₈ inch (1 cm) plus your space distance along from one square end (here, a total of 1¹⁄₈ inches/3 cm). Draw a line across the ribbon at a right angle to the edge at this point. Measure your pleat depth (here, 2¹⁄₄ inches/6 cm) along from the drawn line. Draw another line across the ribbon at this point. Now measure the space distance from this last line, and draw another line. Continue in this way, measuring and marking spaces and pleats until you have measured off the thirteenth pleat and have just the final ³⁄₈ inch (1 cm) seam allowance remaining.

2 To baste the pleats along the drawn lines, lay the ribbon wrong side up. Hand sew a running stitch with the cream thread along each line alternately, creating a zigzag of stitching between the lines, as shown. Gently pull the stitches tight to join the two lines. Baste all the pleats, then check that the pleated ribbon fits snugly around the jacket cuff.

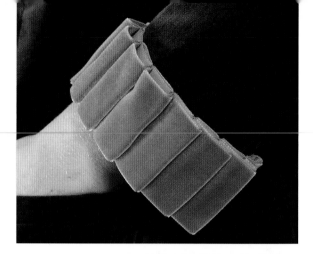

3 Leaving 6-inch (15-cm) long tails of lilac thread at the beginning and end of each line of stitching, machine stitch the pleats along the basting lines. Remove the basting threads.

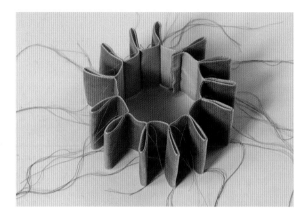

4 Using a ⅜-inch (1-cm) seam allowance, join the ends of the pleated ribbon to form a circle.

6 Slip the pleated cuff over the jacket cuff, so the bottom edges and seams align. Thread the needle with a long length of lilac thread and knot one end. From the inside, bring the needle up through the jacket, next to the edge of the ribbon at the end of one line of machine stitching. Take it down through the edge of the ribbon, over the stitches made in Step 5. Make three or four more stitches in the same way. Slip the needle through the jacket cuff to the next line of machine stitching and repeat until all pleats are tacked down.

5 Fold all the pleats flat in one direction. Thread the needle with one of the tails of thread left in Step 3 and stitch the underside of the pleat to the edge of the line of machine stitching, as shown. Secure the thread on the inside (see Securing Threads, page 9). Repeat around both edges so all of the pleats are stitched down.

7 Stitch the upper edge of the pleated ribbon to the jacket in the same way. Repeat Steps 1–7 to make a second cuff. When you slip it over the sleeve of the jacket, ensure that the pleats are facing in the opposite direction to those on the other cuff, so the two cuffs mirror one another.

gem lapel brooch

Make this pretty brooch to add a little sparkle to your outfit. It is designed to go on the left-hand lapel of a jacket, but if you want to pin it to a right-hand lapel, pleat from the right in Step 9 of the instructions on page 89.

in Step 9 of the instructions on page 89.

you will need

- Diamanté gems with cross-shaped back findings, 6
- Beading needle, size 13
- Beading thread, lilac
- Scissors, embroidery
- Seed beads, size 10, lilac
- Bugle beads, 1/8-inch (4-mm) long, lilac, 12
- Velvet ribbon, 2-inches (5-cm) wide, 6 1/4 inches (16 cm), 1 piece
- Pin back

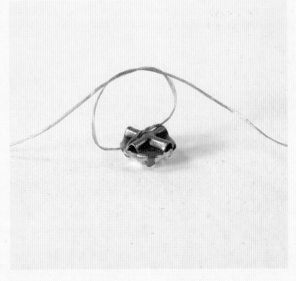

1 Thread the needle with a long length of thread. Take it through the finding on the back of a gem. Leaving a 4-inch (10-cm) tail, knot the thread tightly around the back of the gem with a secure double knot.

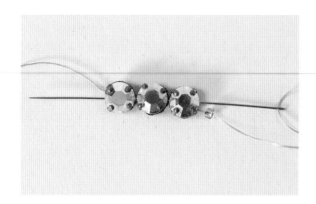

2 Pick up two more gems and one seed bead and return the needle back through the three gems.

5 Pick up a bugle bead and a seed bead and repeat Step 4 until each gem has a seed bead top and bottom and those on one edge are joined with bugle beads.

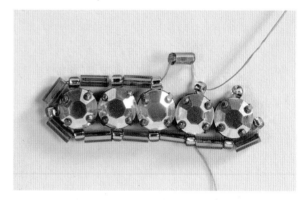

3 Pick up two more gems and another seed bead and return the needle back through all five gems. Take the needle through the first seed bead, all the gems, the second seed bead, and all the gems again. Repeat this several times to ensure that the gems and beads are firmly anchored in a flat, straight band. Finish by coming out through a seed bead.

6 Where there are gaps between seed beads, fill them by taking the needle through the bead, picking up a bugle bead, and taking the needle through the next seed bead. Then, take the needle through all the seed and bugle beads once more and pull on the thread gently to ensure that they are all lying neatly in line.

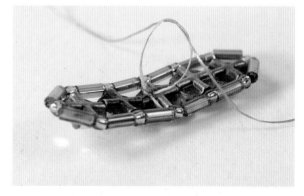

4 Pick up a bugle bead and a seed bead. Take the needle through the finding on the back of the first gem, at right angles to the band. Pick up a seed bead and return the needle through the finding. Take the needle through the first seed bead in the same direction it went through the first time, as shown.

7 Bring the needle through the beads to the center gem and secure the thread by knotting it firmly to the tail of thread left in Step 1. Trim threads short.

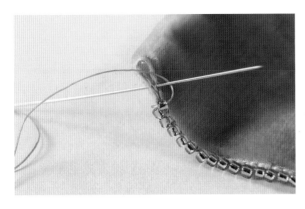

8 Fold over ⅜ inch (1 cm) at one end of the ribbon. Thread the needle with a long length of thread and work beaded blanket stitch (see page 14) along one long edge of the ribbon, catching in the folded end as you stitch. When you are ¾ inch (2 cm) from the other end, fold under ⅜ inch (1 cm) and blanket stitch to the end, catching in the folded-under end, as before.

9 Working from the left-hand end, pleat the edge of the ribbon that isn't beaded to form five equally sized pleats. The width of the pleated edge should be the same as the length of the gem band. Using the beading needle and thread, stitch the pleats in place with tiny whip stitches over the bottom edge

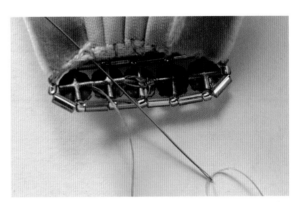

10 Anchor the thread at one end of the ribbon. Take it through the finding on the back of the first gem in the band, then through the edge of the ribbon. Continue in this way until the ribbon is firmly stitched to the gem band.

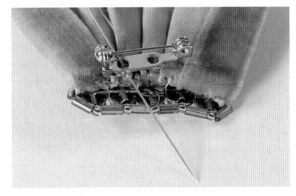

11 Still using the beading needle and thread, sew the pin back to the ribbon where it is attached to the band. Stitch through the backs of the pleats to avoid the thread showing on the front.

trimmed pocket skirt

Update a long skirt by shortening it and using the fabric that is cut off to make a patch pocket. Trim the hem and new pocket with bold, striped ribbon to add eye-catching color and detail.

Long, unlined, green corduroy skirt.

you will need

- Tape measure
- Vanishing fabric marker
- Scissors, dressmaker's
- Iron
- Sewing machine
- Sewing threads, cream, green, and to match outer stripes of ribbon
- Grosgrain ribbon, 2-inches (5-cm) wide, pink, black, cream, orange, green, and red stripes (see How Much?, right)
- Sewing needle (see Needles, page 6)
- Pins

HOW MUCH?

To work out how much ribbon you need, measure around the skirt at the length marked in Step 1. Add ¾ inch (2 cm) for the turn-unders and an additional 6¼ inches (16 cm) for the pocket. If you are going to make the belt as well (see Another Idea, page 93), measure your waist, deduct the width of the belt fastening, and add 1 inch (2 cm) for the turn-unders.

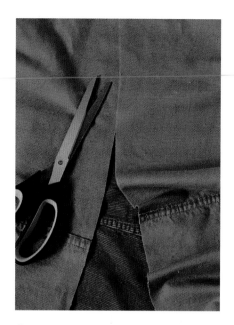

GETTING IT RIGHT

When measuring and marking the skirt prior to cutting off the excess, mark up from the hem at frequent intervals as the hem will probably not be completely straight; it will have a slight curve that you need to duplicate for it to hang well.

1 Decide on the length you want the new skirt to be and add ¾ inch (2 cm) for the hem. (Bear in mind that you need to be able to cut a pocket from the fabric cut off the skirt; see Step 6.) Working on the wrong side, measure up from the existing hem and mark the new length of the skirt (see Getting it Right, above). Cut along the marked line. Set the cut-off fabric aside.

3 Turn under ½ inch (1 cm) at one end of the ribbon and pin it to a side seam, ⅝ inch (1.5 cm) above the folded hem. Pin the ribbon around the bottom of the skirt, keeping it at the same height, and pinning the hem in place at the same time. When you reach the starting point, slip the remaining ½ inch (1 cm) under the turned-under starting end. As the hem of a skirt has a slight curve, pin the lower edge in place first. Then pin the upper edge, easing the ribbon against the fabric for a smooth fit. Baste the ribbon in place along both edges.

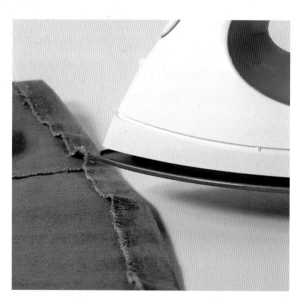

2 Thread the sewing machine with green thread, set it to a medium zigzag stitch, and zigzag around the raw edge. Press under a single ¾-inch (2-cm) hem.

4 Thread the sewing machine with thread to match the ribbon, set it to a medium straight stitch, and sew the ribbon in place along both edges (see Attaching Ribbon, page 12).

5 Using the sewing needle and a thread that matches the ribbon, slip stitch the join between the ends of the ribbon closed.

7 Press under a ⅜-inch (1-cm) hem on the other three sides of the pocket; miter the corners and baste them in place.

8 Position the pocket for best effect on the skirt; pin, then baste it in place. Thread the sewing machine with green thread, set it to a medium straight stitch, and sew the pocket in place around the basted edges, stitching ¼ inch (5 mm) from the fold. Remove the basting threads.

STYLE SOLUTIONS

Here, the patch pocket has been cut with the corduroy lines running in the opposite direction to those on the skirt. The same idea could be used on a striped or patterned fabric to add extra interest to a skirt.

6 Cut a 9½ x 6¼ inch (24 x 16 cm) rectangle from the fabric cut off in Step 1 (see Style Solutions, above). Thread the sewing machine with green thread, set it to a medium zigzag stitch, and zigzag all around the edges. Trim the short top edge of the pocket with ribbon in the same way as the hem of the skirt, pressing under a ¾-inch (2-cm) top hem and sewing on the ribbon. Zigzag stitch across the short ends of the ribbon to attach them to the pocket.

ANOTHER IDEA

If your skirt has self-fabric belt carriers (as this one does), make a simple matching belt from another length of ribbon (see How Much?, page 90). Buy a double-ended belt fastener wide enough to fit the ribbon. Turn under ½ inch (1 cm) at each end of the ribbon. Slip a turned-under end through one side of the fastening and machine stitch it in place, close to the fastener. Repeat for the other end of the ribbon.

ribbon-laced t-shirt

This is a brilliant project that turns a completely ordinary T-shirt into a corset-style lace-up top. There's no hand sewing, so it's quick to do. For another look, turn to page 98 for more lacing ideas.

Sage-green, V-necked, long-sleeved T-shirt.

For another look, turn to page 98 for more lacing ideas.

you will need

Ruler

Vanishing fabric marker

Scissors, dressmaker's

Pins

Grosgrain ribbon, 1-inch (2.5-cm) wide, dark green (see How Much?, below)

Sewing needle (see Needles, page 6)

Sewing machine

Sewing threads, sage green and cream

Silver-colored eyelets, 1/8-inch (3-mm) diameter, 20

Eyelet setting kit

Double-sided satin ribbon, 1/4-inch (6-mm) wide, wine-red, 3 1/4 yards (3 m), 1 piece

HOW MUCH?

You will need two pieces of grosgrain ribbon, each one the length of the front of the T-shirt plus 1 1/4 inches (3 cm).

1 Turn the T-shirt wrong side out and lay it flat on a work surface. Smooth out any wrinkles without stretching the T-shirt out of shape. Using the ruler and fabric marker, mark a straight line down the center front of the T-shirt from neck to hem.

3 Carefully cut the T-shirt up the front, cutting between the zigzagged lines.

2 Set the sewing machine to a narrow zigzag stitch and thread it with the green sewing thread. Without stretching the fabric, machine stitch a line of zigzag stitches ⅛ inch (3 mm) on either side of the drawn line (see Getting it Right, below). Make sure each line of the stitching starts at the top of the neckband and goes to the bottom of the hem.

GETTING IT RIGHT

When stitching on stretchy material, the trick is to let the fabric feed through the machine at its own pace, rather than helping it through as you might with a nonstretch fabric. An ordinary zigzag, as used here, works perfectly well, but if your sewing machine has a special stretch zigzag stitch, then use that.

4 With the wrong-side of the T-shirt up, turn the edge under and pin a ½-inch (1-cm) hem along a zigzagged edge as shown.

5 Turn under ½ inch (1 cm) of one short end of a length of the ribbon. Pin it to the back of the T-shirt along the folded edge and with the turned-under end of the ribbon even with the bottom hem of the T-shirt. Using the cream thread, baste the ribbon in place along the front edge, removing the pins as you stitch. Be careful not to stretch the T-shirt fabric or the finished result will be puckered.

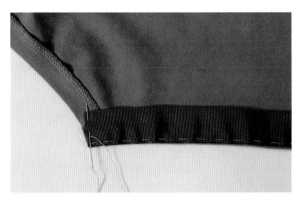

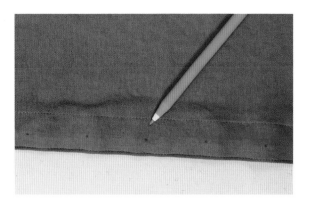

6 Stop basting just before you reach the neck of the T-shirt, but do not secure the thread. Trim the excess ribbon to ½ inch (1 cm) above the neckline. Fold the ribbon end under and baste it to the T-shirt. Secure the thread (see Securing Threads, page 9). Starting at the hem edge, baste the other side of the ribbon in place.

8 With the right-side up, lay one front edge of the T-shirt flat. Using the fabric marker, mark the positions for the eyelets. Place them ½ inch (1 cm) in from the front edge of the top-stitched rectangle, with one eyelet ½ inch (1 cm) from the top and bottom and eight more spaced evenly in between (here, 1¾ inches (4.5 cm apart). Mark the eyelet placements in the same positions on the other T-shirt edge.

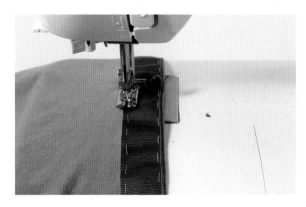

7 Set the sewing machine to a medium straight stitch, and machine stitch the ribbon in place (see Attaching Ribbon, page 12). Stitch as accurately and neatly as you can, because the stitching will show on the front of the T-shirt as a top-stitched rectangle. Secure the threads. Following Steps 4–7, sew the other length of ribbon to the other inside front edge of the T-shirt.

9 Follow the instructions from the eyelet setting kit, setting an eyelet at every marked position.

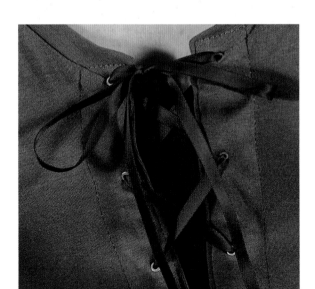

10 Using the satin ribbon and starting at the bottom, lace the two edges of the T-shirt together and tie a bow at the top.

Lacing the T-shirt with different materials can change the look. For a romantic style, use a wide organza ribbon. It is fine enough to thread through the eyelets, if you twist the end into a tight roll.

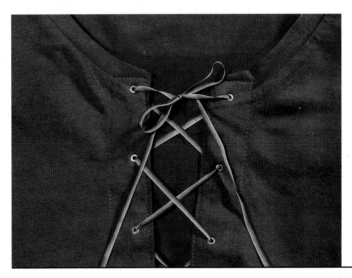

A color-coordinated ribbon (here, a variegated green) looks good, if the T-shirt is worn over a contrasting tank.

Pink string offers a fun way to lace your T-shirt.

sewing

two-into-one t-shirt

This is another project with a practical as well as creative aspect. If one favorite T-shirt has a frayed neck because you've worn it so much and another has a tear on the bottom edge, recycle the good halves to create an original garment, further embellished with simple embroidery.

Pale pink and purple-and-white patterned T-shirts that are the same size.

you will need

- Ruler
- Vanishing fabric marker
- Sewing machine
- Sewing thread, purple
- Scissors, dressmaker's
- Embroidery needle (see Needles, page 6)
- Embroidery floss, purple, 1 skein

STYLE SOLUTIONS
The best places to join the
T-shirts are just below the bust or
at the waist, depending on your
figure. The former works well
if you have a small bust, the latter
will highlight a slim waist.

1 Decide which T-shirt will be the top and which the bottom. Turn the T-shirts wrong-side out and lay them flat on a work surface. Smooth out any wrinkles without stretching the T-shirts out of shape. On the wrong side of both T-shirts, measure up from the hem to the point where the seam will be (see Style Solutions, above). Using the ruler and fabric marker, mark a straight line right around the T-shirts at this point.

2 Set the sewing machine to a narrow zigzag. Without stretching the fabric (see Getting it Right, below), machine stitch along the lines on both T-shirts.

3 Carefully cut the T-shirts in half. On the top T-shirt, cut just below the line and on the bottom one, cut just above the line.

GETTING IT RIGHT

When machine sewing on stretchy material, the trick is to let it feed through the machine at its own pace, rather than helping it through as you might with a nonstretch fabric. An ordinary zigzag, as used here, works perfectly well, but if your sewing machine has a special stretch zigzag stitch, then use that.

You will now have a top and bottom half for your new T-shirt.

4 Right-sides facing, pin the T-shirts together along the zigzagged edges. Place pins at frequent intervals.

5 Set the sewing machine to a medium straight stitch. Using a ½-inch (1-cm) seam allowance, sew the T-shirts together, being careful not to stretch the fabric.

6 Press the seam allowances toward the bottom half of the T-shirt.

7 Thread the needle with a long length of floss and knot one end. Work chain stitch (see page 13) around the seam. Decorate the neckline and cuffs of the T-shirt with the same stitch.

pretty patched trousers

This is a truly creative project that you can easily adapt to suit almost any garment. Raid the scrap bag for some interesting bits of fabric and the button box for a few vintage buttons; visit your local notions store for some sew-on motifs to complement your finds.

Long, pale-pink, linen trousers.

you will need

- Scraps of fabrics (see Style Solutions, page 106)
- Scissors, dressmaker's
- Iron
- Pins
- Embroidery needle (see Needles, page 6)
- Embroidery flosses
- Sewing needle (see Needles, page 6)
- Sew-on motifs
- Sewing threads, to match motifs
- Vintage buttons

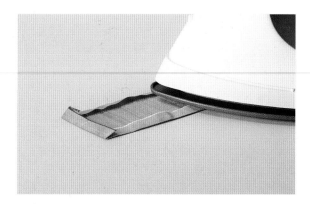

1 Cut the fabrics into squares and rectangles (see Style Solutions, below). Don't worry about making the shapes perfectly regular; part of the charm of this project lies in the naïve finish. Press under a ½-inch (1-cm) seam allowance on all fraying fabrics. (Non-fraying fabrics can be used without seam allowances.)

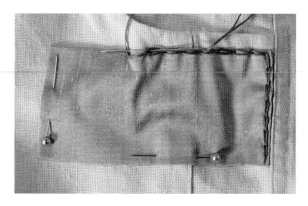

2 One at a time, pin the patches in place. Using the embroidery needle and three strands of floss, sew some patches in place with chain stitch (see page 13). Stitch close to the edge of the patch and be careful not to catch any pocket linings in the stitching.

STYLE SOLUTIONS

There are no real rules for this project, but sticking to a simple color palette and basic shapes will stop the finished garment looking too crazy. Here, pinks and creams have been used to coordinate with the color of the trousers, with a touch of blue as an accent. All the patches are square or rectangular. How you arrange the patches will depend to an extent on your garment. Sewing on fairly small patches (here, they range from 1½ x 2 inches/4 x 5 cm to 2½ x 4 inches\6 x 10 cm) and in groups of two to four works well. I worked in a quite free-form way, sewing on one patch, then positioning the next where it looked best. If you prefer, you can pin on a whole group of patches, and just unpin what is needed to do the embroidery where they overlap. Place groups of patches to highlight existing details on the garment (such as pockets), or where they will show best (for example, on knees and fronts of thighs). Scatter the buttons and sew-on motifs between the patch groups so that they are fairly evenly distributed.

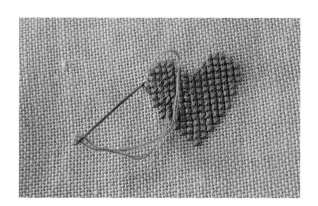

3 If you are a cross-stitcher, you can embroider the heart that is charted on page 125 onto a suitable scrap of fabric. Here, it is embroidered onto even-weave linen.

4 Sew on other patches using running stitch. Make the stitches deliberately uneven to enhance the vintage look.

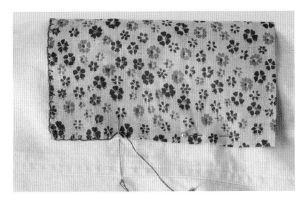

5 Use blanket stitch (see page 14) to sew on yet more patches.

6 Using the sewing needle and matching thread, sew on the motifs. Some types are best attached with small whipstitches around the edges, while others, like these wings, have irregular edges and are best attached with small running stitches within the shape. Sew some motifs onto the garment itself and others onto patches.

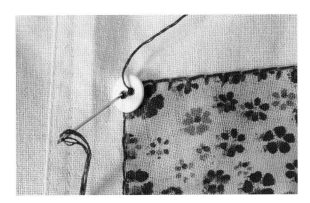

7 Using the embroidery needle and floss, sew on buttons. As well as being decorative, these are very useful for covering up corners where your embroidery has wobbled a little more than you like.

retro furry cardigan

Dig out that boring cardigan that's been hiding in your closet for years and add touches of faux fur to create a modern twist on a fabulously retro 1950s-style top. Both the cute cuffs and little scarf are quick and simple to do, so plan on wearing your new cardigan out tonight.

Fine wool, machine-knit, pale-pink, button-through cardigan.

you will need

FUR CUFFS

Fur fabric, mint-green
  (see How Much?, below)
Sewing machine
Sewing thread, mint green
Scissors, dressmaker's and
  embroidery
Sewing needle (see Needles, page 6)
Pins

HOW MUCH?

For each cuff you need a piece of faux fur the circumference of the cuff plus 1 inch (2.5 cm) by 4 inches (10 cm). Align the pieces with the grain of the fabric. Adding the furry cuffs does stop the knitwear from stretching, and if you stretch the knitted fabric to sew the cuffs on, it tends to pucker unattractively. Therefore, only apply cuffs to sleeves that don't need to stretch to fit over your hands

1 Thread the sewing machine and set it to a medium straight stitch. Right-sides facing, sew the short ends of a fur strip together, taking a ⅜-inch (1-cm) seam allowance.

GETTING IT RIGHT

Faux fur fabric usually has a fairly coarse backing with the grain being very obvious. Therefore, just measure and mark 1¼ inch (3 cm) with a pin, then stitch following the fabric grain.

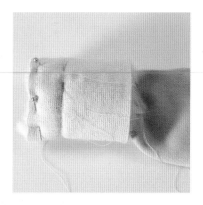

4 Using the sewing needle and doubled thread, backstitch the cuff to the sleeve 1¼ inches (3 cm) up from the bottom edge (see Getting it Right, left).

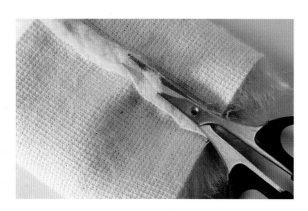

2 Trim the seams to ¼ inch (5 mm). Using the embroidery scissors, trim off as much fur as possible on the seam allowances to avoid bulkiness.

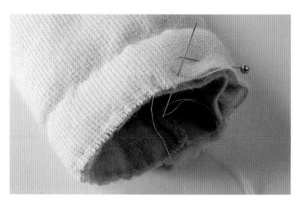

5 Using the sewing needle and doubled thread, whipstitch the bottom edge of the cuff to the hem of the sleeve to prevent it rolling up.

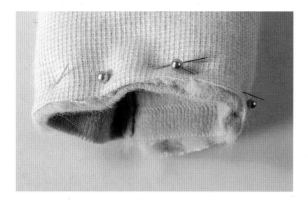

3 With right-sides facing, slip the cuff over a sleeve with the bottom edges and seams aligned, and pin in place. Make sure that the sleeve is not wrinkled inside the fur cuff.

6 Turn the sleeve inside out. Fold the cuff out and back over the hem to the wrong side. Whipstitch the top edge of the cuff to the sleeve, stitching below the line of backstitches. Make the sewing stitches quite deep into the fur to avoid the backing threads of the fur fabric fraying.

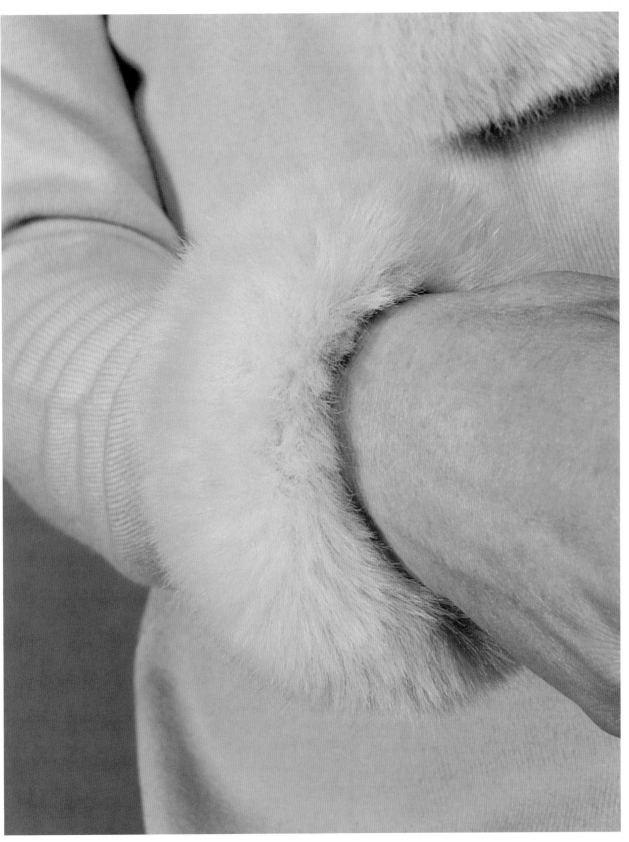

skinny scarf

you will need

- Fur fabric, mint-green, 33 x 4 inches (84 x 10 cm), 1 piece
- Silk fabric, rose pink, 33 x 4 inches (84 x 10 cm), 1 piece
- Pins
- Sewing machine
- Sewing thread, mint green
- Scissors, dressmaker's
- Sewing needle (see Needles, page 6)
- Purchased brooch

1 With right-sides facing, pin the two pieces of fabric together around the edges.

2 Thread the sewing machine and set it to a medium straight stitch. Stitch the fabrics together, using a ⅜-inch (1-cm) seam allowance and leaving a 4-inch (10-cm) opening in the middle of one long side.

3 Trim the corners of the fabric to reduce bulkiness.

4 Turn the scarf right-side out through the gap. Pin then slip stitch the gap closed. Use the brooch to pin the scarf together.

bohemian
skirt

Don't be put off by the amount of machine stitching in this project, as this is one instance where it is not necessary to be very accurate. The lines of stitching can be quite wobbly—it will add to the gypsy look.

Long, flared skirt in soft-sheen, crinkle-finish, purple fabric

you will need

Ruler
Tape measure
Duoppioni silk fabric, pale pink and
    rose pink (see How Much?, below)
Scissors, embroidery
Pins
Sewing machine
Sewing thread, metallic pink
Sewing needle (see Needles, page 6)
Flat sequins, ⅜-inch (1-cm) diameter,
    rose pink, about 350

HOW MUCH?

The strips of fabric are torn from selvedge to selvedge, so the width of the fabric must be at least 2 inches (5 cm) longer than your skirt. You will need about 7 strips of each fabric, each strip 1¼ inches (3 cm) wide, so a total of 8¾ inches (21 cm) of each color fabric. It is always wise to buy more than the minimum in case the fabric was not originally cut on the grain line or you make mistakes.

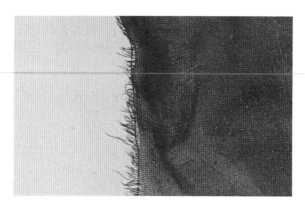

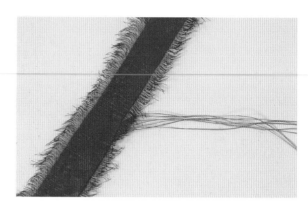

1 Starting from a straight edge, measure and mark seven 1¼-inch (3-cm) intervals along one selvedge edge of both silk fabrics. Make a small, straight cut though the selvedge at each marked point.

3 Fray the strips further by pulling out threads along the torn edges. Fray them to different depths with the central, whole section of fabric ranging from ¾ inch (2 cm) to ⅜ inch (1 cm) wide.

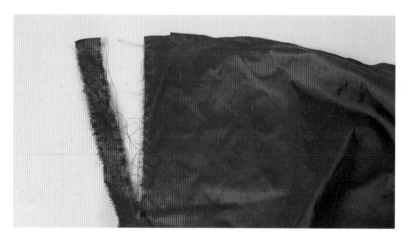

2 Holding the fabric firmly on either side of the cut, tear it along the grain. Move your hands down and continue tearing the full width of the fabric. Don't worry that the fabric puckers as you tear. If necessary, use scissors to snip through the selvedge edge on the other edge of the fabric. Tear seven strips from each fabric color in this way.

GETTING IT RIGHT
Nearly all silk fabrics have a warp thread of one color and a weft thread of another, so when you fray the edge of the fabric the protruding threads may not be the same color as the fabric itself. This color change adds to the bohemian look of the skirt. However, do ask the store to cut you a swatch of your chosen fabric, then fray the edge and check that you like the color of the threads against your garment before buying the full quantity of fabric.

4 Pin the strips around the waistband of the skirt, with ¾ inch (2 cm) of each strip protruding beyond the waistband. Alternate the colors and use different width strips randomly. Space the strips so that the edges of the frayed threads are about ¾ inch (2 cm) apart at the top and ensure that they run in straight lines down the skirt.

6 Thread the sewing machine with the metallic thread and set it to a medium straight stitch. From waistband to hem, sew a line right down the middle of each strip, ensuring that you catch the folded-over end at the top. Reverse a few stitches at the beginning and end of the line of stitching to secure it (see Securing Threads, page 9). Remove the pins as you reach them.

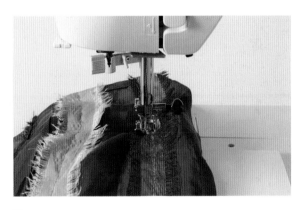

5 Pin the strips in place down the length of the skirt, being careful to keep the strips flat on the fabric to avoid puckering and ensuring that they remain straight. Let the ends of the strips hang loose beyond the hem of the skirt. Fold and pin the end of each strip over the top of the waistband.

7 Sew two more lines down each strip in the same way, but position one at either edge of the central whole section of fabric, to prevent it fraying farther.

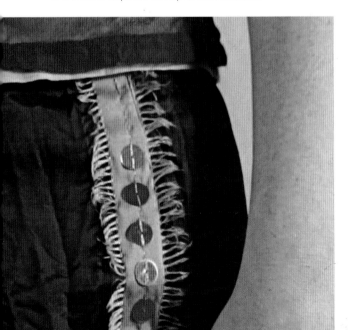

8 Use the eye end of the sewing needle to tease out any stray threads along the edges of the silk strips, then cut them off close to the stitching.

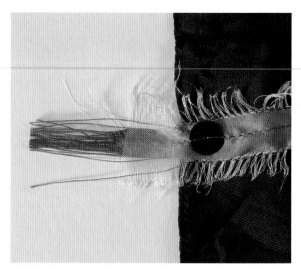

9 Thread the sewing needle with metallic thread and hand stitch about 25 sequins onto each strip. Place them at random intervals, clustering some together, and spacing others farther apart. To attach a sequin, bring the needle up through the fabric and slip on the sequin. Make a stitch over one edge and bring the needle back up through the hole. Make another stitch over the opposite edge.

10 At the hem, trim the fabric strips to about 1¼ inches (3 cm) long. Pull out the threads across the width of the strip to make little tassels.

silky pashmina shawl

This shawl is decorated in the same way as the Bohemian skirt, but the strips are sewn on with plain thread and, instead of being decorated with sequins, each strip has a different vintage button at the bottom. The frayed tassels are trimmed to the length of the existing fringe and mingle attractively with it.

Fine wool, pistachio-green pashmina shawl.

you will need

- Ruler
- Tape measure
- Duoppioni silk fabric, pale blue
- Scissors, embroidery
- Pins
- Sewing machine
- Sewing thread, pale blue
- Sewing needle (see Needles, page 6)
- Vintage buttons, green

leopard jeans

Transform a pair of dull denim jeans by adding deep cuffs and cute patch pockets, both in furry leopard-print fabric. This isn't at all difficult to do: the original pockets provide the templates and the cuffs are simplicity itself, and completely cool.

Straight-legged denim jeans with back patch pockets.

you will need

LEOPARD CUFFS

Leopard-print velvet fabric (see How Much?, below)
Scissors, dressmaker's
Sewing machine
Sewing threads, dark blue and pale ocher
Pins
Iron

HOW MUCH?

Decide how deep you want your cuffs to be; here, they are 6 inches (15 cm). For each cuff you need the depth plus 2¾ inches (7 cm), by the circumference of the hem of the jeans plus 1¼ inches (3 cm).

1 Cut the hems off the bottom of the legs of the jeans. Thread the sewing machine with the blue sewing thread and set it to a medium zigzag stitch. Take off the extension surface of the sewing machine, if it has one, and zigzag around the bottom of each leg.

3 Press the side seams open.

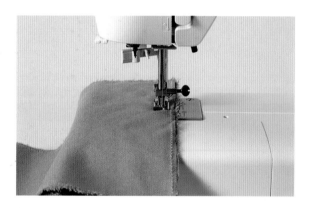

2 Replace the extension surface. Thread the sewing machine with the ocher sewing thread and zigzag around the edges of each cuff piece (see Getting it Right, below). Set the machine to a medium straight stitch. With right-sides facing and using a ⅜-inch (1.2-cm) seam allowance, sew the short side seam of both cuffs.

GETTING IT RIGHT

As velvet frays so easily, zigzagging the edges of the cuff pieces makes them easier to work with. However, if you have chosen to use a different fabric that doesn't fray so easily, you can skip this stage.

4 Turn under ⅝ inch (1.5 cm) around both edges of the tubes and press. Open out flat one of the turned-under edges of each cuff.

5 With the right side of the cuff facing the right side of the leg of the jeans, slip one cuff over a jeans leg, folded-edge first. Align the zigzagged bottom edges and the cuff's side seam with the inside leg seam of the jeans. Pin around the bottom edge. Take off the extension surface of the sewing machine. Using the ocher sewing thread and medium straight stitch, sew the cuff in place, stitching along the pressed line.

6 Turn the jeans inside out. Bring the cuff over the hem of the jeans and up the leg. Pin the folded edge of the cuff to the jeans, ensuring that it is lying flat.

7 Machine stitch the top edge of the cuff to the jeans, sewing close to the folded edge. Repeat Steps 5–7 for the other leg of the jeans.

leopard patch pockets

you will need

- Seam ripper
- Leopard-print velvet fabric, enough to make two pockets the same size as the existing ones
- Pins
- Ruler
- Vanishing fabric marker
- Scissors, dressmaker's
- Sewing machine
- Sewing thread, pale ocher and dark ocher

1 Using the seam ripper, carefully remove the stitches around the edge of each pocket. Remove the pockets and pull out any remaining thread ends.

2 Press open the side and bottom seam allowances of one of the pockets and pin it to the back of the fabric as a pattern. Mark a line across the fabric ¾ inch (2 cm) above the top of the pocket. Cut around the sides and bottom of the pocket and across the marked line.

GETTING IT RIGHT
If you are not the most accurate of machine stitchers, make the new pocket a little bigger than the original one. It will overlap the dark area where the original pocket was and you do not have to be so careful when stitching it in place.

5 Press under the side and bottom edges to create a leopard print pocket that is the same size as the original denim pocket.

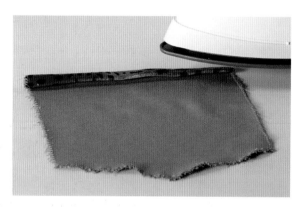

3 Thread the sewing machine with the pale ocher sewing thread and set it to a medium zigzag stitch. Zigzag around the sides and bottom edges of each pocket. Press under a double ⅜-inch (1-cm) hem across each top edge.

6 Pin and baste the new pocket in the position of the original pocket (this will usually be visible as a dark area on the fabric).

4 Thread the sewing machine with the topstitch thread and set it to a medium straight stitch. For each pocket, sew the hem, sewing just under ½ inch (1 cm) from the top edge.

7 Machine stitch both the pockets to the jeans, stitching ¼ inch (5 mm) from the edges.

love t-shirt page 39

flower tank page 32

pretty patched trousers page 104

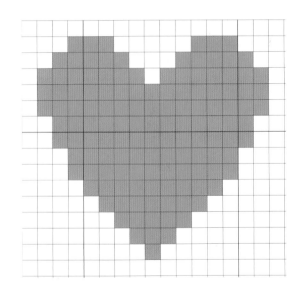

templates

On this page, you will find the templates used in the book. Photocopy your chosen template, or scan it into your computer, enlarging it to suit the size of your garment. Complete instructions on how to use the diagram for the cuff on the Velvet Jacket can be found on pages 84–86.

velvet jacket page 84

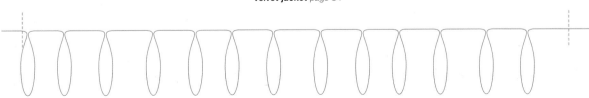

Suppliers

Visit your local or online needlework stores for the products used in this book. If you are unable to locate a store in your area, contact the companies directly.

The Caron Collection
55 Old South Ave.
Stratford, CT 06615
(203) 381-9999
www.caron-net.com; mail@caron-net.com

Coats and Clark
PO Box 12229
Greenville, SC 29612-0229
(800) 648-1479
www.coatsandclark.com

DMC Corporation
South Hackensack Ave.
Port Kearny Bldg. 10 F
South Kearny, NJ 07032
www.dmc.com; dmcusa@dmc.fr

JHB International Inc.
1955 South Quince St.
Denver, CO 80231
(303) 751-8100
www.buttons.com

Mill Hill Beads
Division of Wichelt Imprts Inc.
N162 Hwy. 35
Stoddard, WI 54658
(800) 356-9516www.kolo.com

Pearsall's Embroidery Silk
Tristan Brooks Designs
182 Green Glade Rd.
Memphis, TN 38120-2218
(901) 767-8414
www.tristanbrooks.com;
info@tristanbrooks.com

Rainbow Gallery
7412 Fulton Ave., #5
North Hollywood, CA 91605
(818) 982-6406
www.rainbowgallery.com

The Thread Gatherer
2108 Norcrest Dr.
Boise, ID 83705
(208) 387-2641
www.threadgatherer.com

YLI Corporation
161 West Main St.
Rock Hill, SC 29730
(803) 985-3100
www.ylicorp.com;
ylicorp@ylicorp.com

INDUSTRY RESOURCES

Use the contact information below to locate a shop, refine or learn a new technique, join a guild, or learn about the needlework industry and community.

ANG
American Needlepoint Guild Inc.
PO Box 1027
Cordova, TN 38088-1027
www.needlepoint.org;
membership@needlepoint.org

EGA
Embroiderer's Guild of America
335 West Broadway, Ste. 100
Louisville, KY 40202-2105
(502) 589-6956
www.egausa.org;
egahq@egausa.org

TNNA
The National NeedleArts Association
PO Box 3388
Zanesville, OH 43702-3388
(740) 455-6773
www.tnna.org;
tnna.info@offinger.com

AUTHOR'S ACKNOWLEDGMENTS
My thanks to Paula Breslich and Janet Ravenscroft at Breslich & Foss for offering me such a great project, and for their support at the tricky moments. Thanks to Matthew Dickens for his creative input and ever-excellent photography, and to Janet James for making the pages look delicious. Thanks to Anna Harvey Williams and Amy Dickens for fashion ideas, and to Amy for modeling some of the end results.

Index

As many materials and techniques are used throughout the book, the page references are intended to direct the reader to substantial entries only. Page numbers in *italics* refer to illustrations.